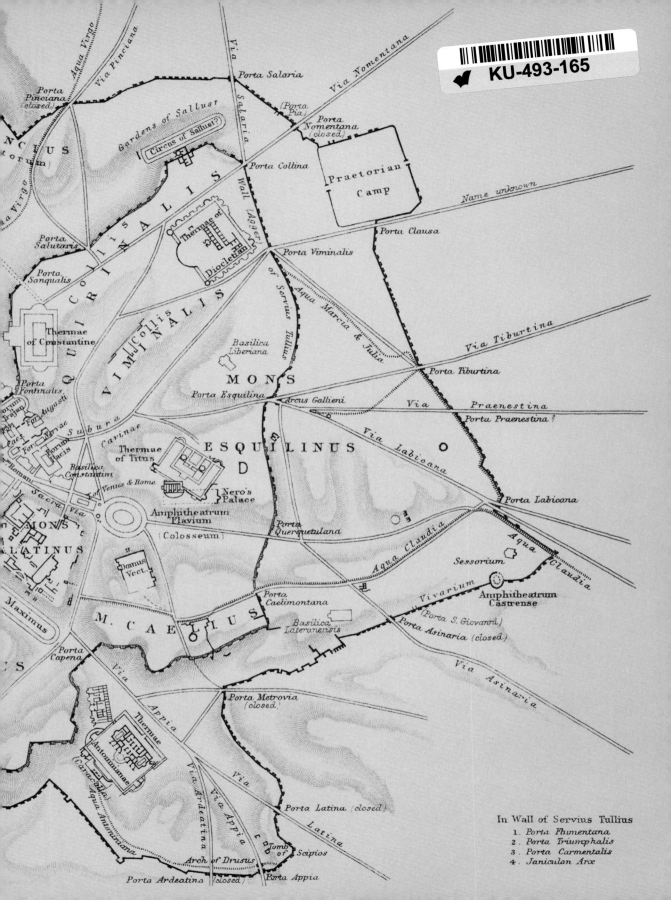

Porta Pinciana (closed)

Aqua Virgo

Via Pinciana

Via Salaria

Porta Salaria

Via Nomentana

Gardens of Sallust

(Porta Pia)

Porta Nomentana (closed)

Circus of Sallust?

Porta Collina

Praetorian Camp

Name unknown

Wall (agger)

Porta Clausa

Porta Salutaris

Thermae of Diocletian

Porta Viminalis

QUIRINALIS

Porta Sanqualis

of Servius Tullius

Aqua Marcia & Julia

Via Tiburtina

VIMINALIS

Collis

Thermae of Constantine

Basilica Liberiana

Porta Tiburtina

Porta Fontinalis

MONS

Via Praenestina

For. Trajani

Forum Augusti

Porta Esquilina

Arcus Gallieni

Via Labicana

Porta Praenestina ?

For. Nervae

Subura

Carinae

ESQUILINUS

Forum Pacis

Basilica Constantini

Thermae of Titus

Porta Labicana

Forum Romanum

Con. Venus & Rome

Nero's Palace

D

Sacra Via

Amphitheatrum Flavium (Colosseum)

Aqua Claudia

Sessorium

Aqua Claudia

MONS PALATINUS

Domus Vect.

Porta Querquetulana

Vivarium

Amphitheatrum Castrense

Maximus

M. CAELIUS

Porta Caelimontana

Basilica Lateranensis

(Porta S. Giovanni)

Porta Asinaria (closed)

Via Asinaria

Porta Capena

Via Appia

Porta Metrovia (closed)

Thermae Antoninianae (Caracalla)

Aqua Antoniniana

Via Ardeatina

Via Appia

Via Latina

Porta Latina (closed)

Arch of Drusus

Tomb of Scipios

Porta Ardeatina (closed)

Porta Appia

In Wall of Servius Tullius
1. Porta Flumentana
2. Porta Triumphalis
3. Porta Carmentalis
4. Janiculan Arx

ANCIENT ROME
IN FIFTY
MONUMENTS

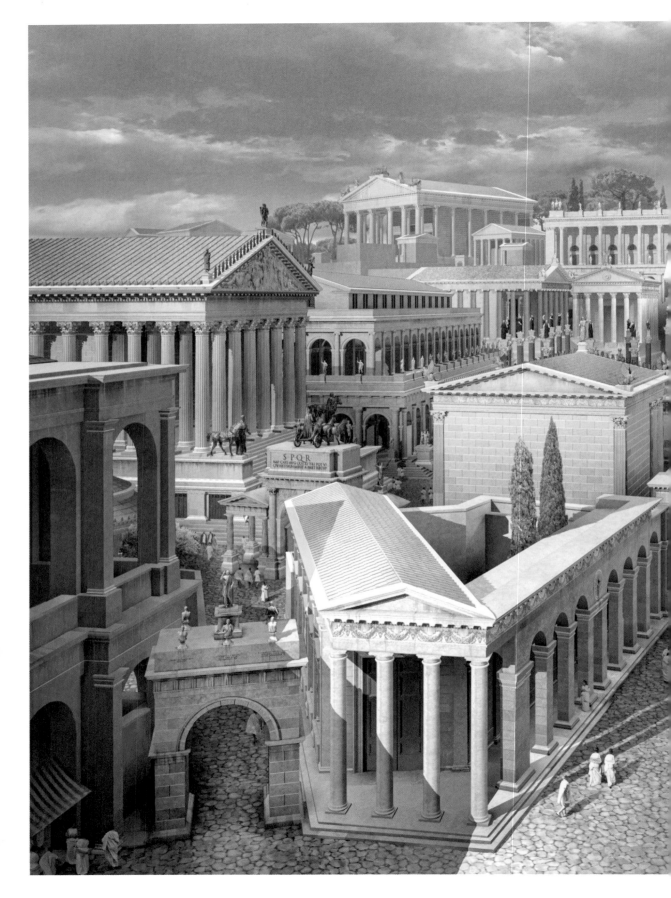

PAUL ROBERTS

ANCIENT ROME

IN · FIFTY

MONUMENTS

CONTENTS

THE MONUMENTS THAT MADE ROME

ROME, AS WE ALL KNOW, was not built in a day: it took centuries. Its evolution was driven by the city's rulers, in particular the emperors, by political and social circumstances, and by the changing technology and materials available. This, together with frequent and devastating fires, meant that Rome was continuously changing and evolving. The imperial city of Augustus in around AD 10 would, in the range and beauty of its public buildings, have been largely unrecognizable to Julius Caesar only fifty years earlier; while Maxentius's city in AD 310 contained vast, concrete-based structures that Augustus could not have dreamt of. Only around the time of Constantine in the AD 320–30s would it have been possible to visit most of the monuments discussed here at the same time.

In Roman life and society, much revolved around the conspicuous display of wealth – and thus, it followed, power. Rome's kings and then its Republican leaders embraced the principle, but the emperors perfected it. The Roman people, according to the 1st-century AD satirist Juvenal, needed, apart from bread, just one thing to keep them happy – circuses: the races, the games. Of almost equal importance to the entertainments were the venues they were held in. When the crowds urged on their favourite chariot team in the huge, beautiful Circus Maximus, or roared at the combats in the gigantic, echoing Colosseum, there was a complex game of identity and power at play between the emperor and the people.

The monuments built by the emperors were a symbol of that power. Construction of these buildings was, as the archaeologist and historian Amanda Claridge underlined, 'a political act: it mattered a great deal who built what and when'. But monuments also helped to empower the populace, fostering a strong sense of *romanitas* – Romanness – and great civic pride. As Pliny commented on the Circus Maximus, built by that 'greatest Prince' the emperor Trajan, this and other buildings were 'worthy of the race that has conquered so many peoples'. In this book, we look, therefore, both at the monuments themselves and at the people who built and used them. We hear their stories, using these extraordinary buildings, as well as ancient literary sources, as pathways not just to the emperors but also to the Roman people.

Of course, Rome was exceptional among all cities. Virgil stated that Rome lifted her head 'above them all, as a cypress tree towers above the rambling bushes'. No other city in the Empire – not even Constantinople – came close to Rome in its prime: not in its size, nor its population, nor the sheer

ROME LIFTED HER HEAD 'ABOVE THEM ALL, AS A CYPRESS TREE TOWERS ABOVE THE RAMBLING BUSHES'

VIRGIL

complexity and diversity of its architectural landscape. In this landscape there were some buildings that only the elite would see, such as the palaces on the Palatine Hill, which still left a great impression even on those who could only read about them. But it was in the building of monuments that people saw and used in their everyday lives that true kudos and power lay. And Rome's public areas were filled with monuments that meant something to its people. There was no such thing in Rome as 'just another temple'. Each monument had a significance – a commemoration of a specific event, an individual or a concept linked to them. In an age without mass media, these public spaces and the monuments they contained were immensely important.

For the fifty monuments that are brought together here, I try to suggest some answers to important questions not always considered today. Why were they built? What did they add to the lives of the people who used them – or the people who built them? What impact did they have on the city and its monumental (and daily) life? What did they look like then, and why do they look the way they do now? This book is an attempt to tell the story, rather than just the history, of the monuments of Rome.

The very word 'monument' comes from the Latin word *monere*, which can mean to remind, to bring to your recollection. The English word 'memorial' serves a similar function, with its obvious links to 'memory'. So monuments have the ability to trigger thoughts and evoke memories, serving as links between the past and the present. These buildings, with their numerous inscriptions and statues, proclaimed loud and clear the messages that the people who had them built wanted the populace to hear. Often, the importance of the monument lies not in the structure itself, but in the political, social or cultural developments that were behind it, and of which it may today represent the best – or only surviving – reflection.

In trying to recreate the story of Rome and its buildings, it is important to look at as full a range of sources as possible. Archaeology is crucial, with the results of excavations and surveys serving as a control for the fascinating literary accounts that have survived. Some recent excavations around the monuments are mentioned, though these are necessarily selective and, given the level of activity in Rome, still more will soon have been uncovered about the sites. This all enables us to piece together a picture of how the monuments arrived in the state we now see them in, and also to fill in the gaps in other sources of our knowledge.

That knowledge is, fortunately, very rich. For much of the Roman period, we have a mass of written evidence: not only from inscriptions, coins and civic calendars, but also from Roman writers – historians, satirists, poets and encyclopaedists – who shine valuable light on the monuments and those who built and used them. From their works, we can gain a sense of the power and impact of the monuments in their prime.

Countless books have been written on ancient Rome: from encyclopaedic archaeological accounts, such as those of Amanda Claridge and Filippo Coarelli (which remain the best sources of their type), to guidebooks for travellers passing through the Eternal City. The way that we look at Rome's monuments is changing all the time in the light of archaeological discoveries and scholarly research, and thus it is always desirable to see whether and how the many pieces of the wonderful puzzle that is Rome can be assembled in new and useful ways.

This book is not a guide to all the monuments of Rome – and it cannot encompass more than a part of this amazing city. The focus here is on fifty monuments found within Rome's still impressive walls, ranging from theatres and temples to baths and bridges. All are accessible to the public, without special permit (though most are ticketed). They range in date from around 600 BC, when Rome was ruled by kings, to the early AD 600s, with the extinguishing of distinctly ancient Roman concepts of urban life and the clear ascendance of the new realities of the early Middle Ages. Let us now look at these rulers and their monumental creations, to try to understand both Rome and the Romans a little better.

A reconstruction of the Forum Romanum in the 4th century AD, looking towards the Capitoline Hill and the Temple of Jupiter Optimus Maximus. The central piazza was originally framed by basilicas and a handful of temples. Over time more monuments were added including the Arch of Septimius Severus and a row of honorary columns and equestrian statues. The heart of Rome was the most monumentalized place of all.

I.

BEGINNINGS

THE KINGDOM OF ROME

(753–509 BC)

ACCORDING TO LEGEND, Rome was founded by Romulus, a descendant of Prince Aeneas of Troy, in 753 BC (on 21 April, to be precise). In reality, at that time, a visitor would not have seen a Classical city with paved streets, fine houses and public buildings, but fortified collections of huts scattered over Rome's hills. Romulus was the first of Rome's seven kings. Some, like Romulus, are lost in legend; others are attested historical figures, and at least two were aristocrats from the wealthy, powerful Etruscan cities north of Rome. But Rome itself, though in legend founded by Trojans, and sometimes ruled by Etruscans, was a city of the Latin people.

Rome was one of many Latin cities, but because of its position at the crossroads of important trade routes and a navigable river, the Tiber, it boomed. It was during the period of Rome's kings that the city's disparate parts were brought together, its site drained through the Cloaca Maxima, its forum, which would become the Forum Romanum, laid out, and its first major public buildings constructed, in particular the great Temple of Jupiter Optimus Maximus.

Towering over the city, the **TEMPLE OF JUPITER OPTIMUS MAXIMUS** (Jupiter Best and Greatest) was Rome's most prominent and most important temple. It was also known as the Capitolium (or Capitol) and gave its name to the Capitoline Hill on which it stood. Even the late Roman writer Ammianus Marcellinus stated in the AD 360s that this temple was the finest building in the world.

Jupiter Optimus Maximus was at the heart of Roman life, society and identity. Rome's senators held the first meeting of the year there, and it was to this temple that generals and, later,

Right: A reconstruction of the Temple of Jupiter Optimus Maximus or Capitolium. Today it has vanished so completely that only parts of its gigantic foundations remain.

Below: The image of the legendary she-wolf suckling the future founders of Rome, Romulus and Remus, has been iconic since Roman times. This bronze sculpture was given to the city by the Pope in 1471, and the babies were added then, but the wolf's age is controversial: usually thought to be 5th-century BC Etruscan, recent scientific analysis suggests a possible medieval origin.

emperors processed in the great triumphs that marked Rome's conquest of the Mediterranean.

The Temple was started as a major project by Rome's kings in the late 600s BC, and no expense was spared in its construction. The finest (that is, Etruscan) masons and sculptors in bronze and terracotta were employed. Completed by Tarquin II (the Proud), the last king of Rome, it was dedicated in 509 BC under the new Republic, after Tarquin's expulsion.

This immense structure covered an area of around 55 × 70 m (180 × 230 ft), and much of the Capitoline Hill had to be levelled to accommodate it. It was very Etruscan in style (unsurprising, perhaps, given its regal Etruscan builders), with a deep front porch, a forest of columns and a frontal staircase. Its precinct was filled with statues, shrines and dedications, while the Temple itself was richly decorated with statues and plaques in polychrome terracotta – an Etruscan speciality. Even the cult statue of Jupiter, created by the expert Etruscan craftsman Vulca, was made of painted terracotta.

The *cella* (inner sanctum) was divided into three parts, with Jupiter at the centre, his wife and queen Juno left, and daughter Minerva right – the 'Capitoline triad'. The Temple was finely adorned. The floor of the *cella* was of fine white mosaic – incredibly, its first large-scale use in Rome. In 146 BC, gold from the conquered city of Carthage was used to gild the Temple's ceiling – another first – and later the bronze tiles of the roof were also gilded. The Temple of Jupiter reflected how Roman society was getting richer and more ostentatious thanks to its conquests. The writer Seneca pointed out the consequence of this sudden and massive wealth, commenting wryly that

'THINGS WERE QUIET WHEN WE WERE POOR, BUT ONCE WE GILDED THE ROOF OF THE CAPITOL, THE CIVIL WARS BEGAN'

SENECA

TRIUMPHS

TRIUMPHS WERE SPECTACULAR, theatrical, colourful processions led by a victorious general in his chariot, his face painted red to imitate the early statues of Jupiter himself. They displayed for all to see the glorious spoils of war – gold and silver coins and bullion, sculptures, paintings, even luxurious furniture and tapestries. And of course the spoils included enslaved people: the leaders of the defeated peoples and their families; workers for Rome's fields, mines and homes; but also specialists in sculpture, painting, architecture and even cooking. All of this began to transform Roman society.

Previous pages: C.R. Cockerell, *Imaginary View of the Temple of Jupiter Capitolinus, Rome*. The heart of sacred life, the repository of Rome's early records, the destination of triumphant generals, the Capitolium encapsulated Roman identity.

Above: The Capitoline triad of Jupiter, Juno and Minerva (with their sacred birds, eagle, peacock and owl). The three gods were venerated in the Temple of Jupiter Optimus Maximus.

'things were quiet when we were poor, but once we gilded the roof of the Capitol, the Civil Wars began'.

The Temple held many treasures – dedications in gold and silver, an archive of bronze tablets charting Rome's conquests and treaties and, most importantly, the Sibylline Books. These were sacred texts bought by King Tarquin I from the priestess, or Sibyl, of Apollo at Cumae, near Naples. They were to be consulted over important decisions and at times of danger, but sadly did not predict their own destruction when the Temple burned down in 83 BC. The dictator Sulla rebuilt it, using columns from the unfinished Temple of Zeus in Athens (underlining where power lay now), and later the first emperor, Augustus, sourced a replacement set of the Books. He transferred them to his Temple of Apollo on the Palatine Hill for safekeeping – and he was right to be cautious.

The Temple was destroyed again in AD 69 in the chaotic power struggle after the death of Nero, and the emperor Vespasian's rebuilding of the temple was itself consumed by fire in AD 80. But the next rebuilding, by the emperor Domitian

Opposite: Relief from a triumphal arch of Marcus Aurelius, showing the emperor preparing to sacrifice to Jupiter. He stands before a stylized representation of the Temple of Jupiter: there are too few columns, but the temple with its three great gates is clearly intended.

Overleaf: A view of the Cloaca Maxima where it flowed into the Tiber by Giovanni Battista Piranesi, 1748–78. The Cloaca Maxima was key to keeping the area from the Forum Romanum to the Forum Boarium (visible above, with its Temple of Hercules Victor) drained and practicable.

in the late 80s, outlasted the Empire. This version was made of fine Athenian Pentelic marble, in rich and splendid imperial Corinthian style, with gilded doors and roof tiles. It was as gigantic as its predecessors, with columns over 20 m (65½ ft) high, and in the *cellae* were colossal chryselephantine (ivory and gilded bronze) statues of the three gods.

Closed in the AD 390s, the Temple stood intact until AD 455, when the Germanic Vandals pillaged Rome and carried off the gilded tiles. It was restored – for its civic symbolism, not for its (now forbidden) religious importance – but in 571 the Byzantine governor of Rome removed any remaining statues, and the Temple vanishes from record until a writer in the 1100s briefly mentions its ruins. During the 16th and 17th centuries, colossal columns and other elements of architecture were found, so immense that even small elements were used to carve whole statues, for example those in the church of Santa Maria della Pace.

Only fragments of the Temple remains above ground, but in the great glazed courtyard of the Capitoline Museums is a mass of tufa foundation blocks. This is a small portion of the original footings, but still so extensive that, when archaeologists excavated the area in the 1990s, they believed they had found an enormous piazza.

Much less glamorous than the Temple of Jupiter, but essential for Rome's successful expansion into the areas between its hills, was the main drain or **CLOACA MAXIMA**. It was built by the kings in the late 500s BC and ran from the Subura slum district to the River Tiber, via the Forum Romanum and the Forum Boarium (Cattle Market). The drain's main function was initially to channel water from Rome's low-lying areas, though it was also connected to storm drains and later carried waste water from some major public buildings such as baths and theatres.

Most private homes or apartment blocks (*insulae*) were not linked to the Cloaca Maxima, relying instead on chamber pots and cesspits. As with all areas of Roman life, a god protected the drain. Surprisingly, perhaps, it was Venus, goddess of love and beauty. In the Forum Romanum there was even a small sanctuary to Venus Cloacina (Venus of the Drain). The kings made the channel of the drain wide enough for a hay-laden cart to pass through, while Marcus Agrippa, the deputy and son-in-law of Augustus, having restored the drain, inspected it by sailing through it in a boat.

V E D U T A delle antiche Sostruzioni fatte da Tarquinio Superbo dette il Bel Lido, o come altri erette da Marco Agrippa a' tempi di
Augusto, in occasione, ch' Egli fece ripurgare tutte le Cloache, fino al Tevere. A Sbocco della Cloaca Massima al medesim.

B *Tempio di Cibele, o come altri d'Ercole, il quale era situato nell'antico Foro Boario.*   C *Avanzi delle antiche*
D *Monistero e Chiesa di S. Alessio.*   E *Priorato della Sagra Religione di Malta.*   *Saline.*

Cav. Piranesi F.

THE REPUBLIC

(509–31 BC)

I N 509 BC TARQUIN II was expelled from the city, and Rome became a Republic with two joint heads of state: the consuls, supported by the Senate and by the people of Rome, i.e. *Senatus Populusque Romanus*. The initials SPQR became a powerful emblem on official inscriptions and public buildings. During the 500-year period of the Republic, Rome was transformed from an important regional centre into the most powerful city then known. Rome first made allies of (or conquered) its fellow Latin cities and then expanded further into central Italy, conquering peoples such as the Samnites and the Etruscans. By around 200 BC, it had conquered most of the Italian peninsula and islands, and only a century later, controlled most of the Mediterranean. The year 146 BC was particularly momentous, with the destruction in the Eastern Mediterranean of the leader of the Greek cities, Corinth, and in the west, the final extinction of the mighty city of Carthage.

For most of the Republic, Rome was involved in almost incessant wars – local, national, international and civil. It certainly needed its imposing walls (not those surrounding the city today, which date to the AD 270s). These wars had a great impact on Rome – in particular through all the power and wealth that victory brought. The enormous quantities of money, slaves and works of art that poured into Rome were culturally and artistically transformative, but became points of envy and discord, both among wealthy senators and generals, and between these and the less privileged classes. Eventually these tensions would lead to civil wars that would tear the Republic apart.

For much of the Republic, Rome's monuments were not particularly numerous or (Jupiter Optimus Maximus aside)

DURING THE 500-YEAR PERIOD OF THE REPUBLIC, ROME WAS TRANSFORMED INTO THE MOST POWERFUL CITY THEN KNOWN

A view across Largo Argentina showing the temple complex revealed when medieval and Renaissance buildings were cleared in the 1920s. The two temples in the foreground were found still standing, while excavations revealed two more temples and some other structures.

particularly grand, certainly when compared with many Greek cities. The focus tended to be on temples, because the gods and, as importantly, the rituals around their worship were absolutely fundamental to Roman life. Temples were often built in groups, as seen in Largo Argentina, in contrast to the later and grander imperial stand-alone temples in their colonnades and piazzas. They were built as votives of thanks for victories in Rome's endless wars – especially against Carthage or enemies in Italy or the Greek east – or as pleas for the gods' protection against other threats, such as plague.

But from around the 180s/170s BC Rome's landscape began to change. Wealth, slaves (including skilled workers and craftsmen) and increased know-how flowing in from conquered lands resulted in new and ever more expensive and ambitious building programmes. Temples were still a focus, but they were now built of increasingly costly materials, such as the Parian marble of the Temple of Hercules Victor. Other temples or groups of temples, such as Largo Argentina, were rebuilt, repaved and embellished. In another example of Greek influence, types of Hellenistic monuments quite new to Rome began to

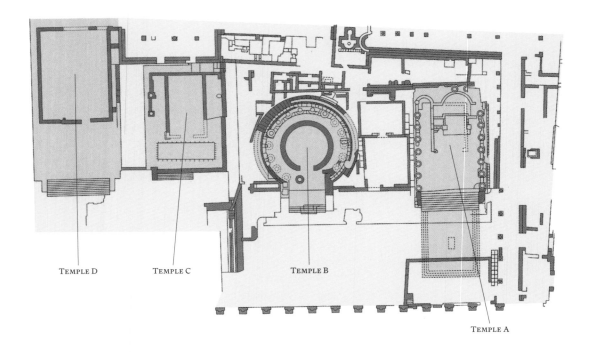

TEMPLE D   TEMPLE C   TEMPLE B

TEMPLE A

appear, such as colonnaded porticoes and the first versions of
aisled basilicas (law courts and financial centres).

The wealthy had always led in building projects, but this
became even more marked in the last century of the Republic
as leaders such as Sulla, Pompey and Julius Caesar increasingly
used monuments to bolster their status and further their
political aims.

The best surviving group of Republican temples is in the
traffic-filled square of **LARGO ARGENTINA**, which was an intact
medieval cityscape, with towers, palaces and churches, until 1926
when Mussolini's demolition men moved in. It was an important
centre of ancient Roman religion, with as many as six temples,
one of the largest such complexes in the city, making it a major
focal point, a generator of sacred energy. The four now visible
were first built in the 3rd to 2nd centuries BC, with subsequent
remodelling seen in the different types of masonry and levels
of paving. In 2023, the area of the four temples, conserved and
made much more comprehensible, opened to the public. A display
of finds from the site includes the heads of two colossal statues.

Inscriptions, sculptures and mentions by Roman writers
allow a tentative identification of the temples, usually referred

Above: Map showing the
temple complex in Largo
Argentina. The gods of
Temples A–D are likely to
be, from right to left, Juturna,
goddess of springs, Fortuna
Huiusce Diei (Fortune of
This Day), Feronia and the
Lares Permarini, the guardians
of sailors. Behind Temple B
are the remains of the Theatre
of Pompey's Curia, where
Caesar was assassinated.

Opposite, top: The head
of Fortuna Huiusce Diei, found
near Temple B. It was probably
part of its cult statue with the
marble head and limbs
attached to a torso of wood,
covered with gilded bronze.

IT WAS HERE THAT ON THE IDES OF MARCH 44 BC CAESAR DIED AT THE FEET OF POMPEY'S STATUE

Right: Church of San Nicola in Carcere in which the columns of the Temple of Hope are clearly visible. This temple was one of a group of four Republican temples that once stood near the river in the Forum Holitorium.

to (unromantically) as Temples A–D. The rectangular Temple A (on the viewer's far right) was dedicated in the 250s/240s BC to Juturna, a goddess of springs and the sister of the patrons of Rome, Castor and Pollux. Its rough brown-green tufa columns were once coated with sparkling white stucco. Temple B, reflecting the Greek fashion for round structures or *tholoi*, was dedicated around 100 BC by Lutatius Catulus, a military and political leader whose son rebuilt the Temple of Jupiter Optimus Maximus. A colossal head of Fortuna, 1.5 m (5 ft) high, was found next to it, suggesting the temple honoured Fortuna Huiusce Diei (Fortune of This Day), whose temple was known to be here. Originally, her head and limbs were attached to a torso of wood covered with gilded bronze. Temple B was also an art gallery, with a 5th-century BC statue of Athena by the great Pheidias, the sculptor of the statues of Zeus at Olympia and Athena in the Parthenon in Athens.

Religion and ordinary life sat side by side, and the small building between Temples A and B was probably the Statio Aquarum – the headquarters of the officials who ran the city's water supply. Temple C was perhaps dedicated to Feronia, an ancient Italic goddess linked to Juno, with terracotta decoration dating to the 290s/280s BC making it the oldest of the four. Temple D, partly buried under the modern piazza, was by far the largest (though its modern claim to fame is that it houses the largest cat sanctuary in Rome).

Traces survive of the colonnaded square behind the Theatre of Pompey, which backed on to the sacred precinct. Behind

Temple A is a long, narrow *latrina* or public toilet, with no cubicles or partition walls (modern ideas of privacy weren't Roman). Behind Temple B are the jumbled foundations of a large hall, where the Senate met after the Curia (Senate House) in the Forum Romanum was burned down by rioters in 52 BC. It was here that on the Ides (15) of March 44 BC Caesar died at the feet of Pompey's statue. Strange to think that on this spot, where buses and trams hurtle by, history changed forever.

The precinct began to change in the 5th century AD. Temples C and D lost their columns, to be used in new churches, and the area became the property of a monastery. From the early 900s, Temple A became a church; medieval frescoes and crudely

A lively reconstruction of the Forum Boarium with the cattle that gave the Forum its name. On the left is the rectangular Temple of Portunus (god of ports), overlooking the nearby river port, and in the right foreground is the Temple of Hercules Victor. As patron of flocks and herdsmen, Hercules had strong links to the Forum.

added apses remain today. Its name – San Nicola de Calcarario (St Nicholas of the Lime-Kiln) – is a chilling reminder of the fate of the temples' marble architecture and decoration. Sadly, the lime-kilns in the area worked for centuries.

There are other Republican temples still extant in Rome. At the foot of the Capitoline Hill, there were four temples in an area called the Forum Holitorium, or vegetable market. They were built between the 250s and 190s BC to gain the gods' favour during wars with Carthage and other enemies. Parts of three temples Spes (Hope), Juno Sospita (Juno the Saviour) and Janus were eventually incorporated into the church of San Nicola in Carcere.

Another group of temples and shrines grew up at the foot of the Palatine Hill, in an area that was not a temple precinct but a working area called the Forum Boarium – literally the cattle market. It was a major crossroads and emporium, and a river port with wharves and warehouses was found in the 1920s. Cattle were traded here, as drove animals, for food and as sacrificial offerings in Rome's many cults, and the Forum was also a financial centre for those involved in the industry.

The area had a strong link with the demi-god Hercules – and cattle. In myth, the hero rested by the Tiber after performing his Tenth Labour (stealing the cattle of the monster Geryon in Spain). While he slept, the ogre Cacus stole the cattle, dragging them backwards so they left no followable trail. Hercules was not fooled, killed Cacus, then built the great altar of Hercules on the site and promptly sacrificed the just-liberated cattle. Other shrines and temples followed and the whole area became sacred to him.

Above: The Temple of Hercules Victor, c. 140s BC, was among the first temples in Rome to be made completely of marble. The upsurge in wealth from Rome's conquest of the Mediterranean increasingly changed the cityscape.

Opposite: Gilded bronze statue of Hercules, discovered in the Forum Boarium in the 1470s. Its striking level of preservation implies it was deliberately buried in antiquity.

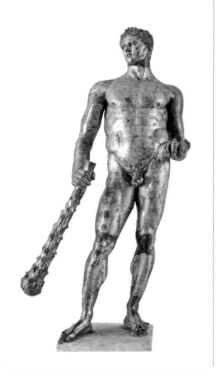

Near the rectangular Temple of Portunus, god of ports, is a near-intact round temple, almost certainly the **TEMPLE OF HERCULES VICTOR** or Hercules Olivarius, after the area's olive oil traders. At about 15 m (49 ft) in diameter, it is approximately the same size as the Temple of Vesta in the Forum Romanum, which gives an idea of that temple's appearance. Built in the mid-2nd century BC, Hercules Victor was restored many times – in particular in AD 15 by the emperor Tiberius after a devastating flood. It is round, in Greek style, but its real importance lies in its materials. It was one of the first temples in Rome to be built largely of marble, most of it expensive white Pentelic marble from Athens. It may even have been imported in pieces to Rome then assembled by Greek craftsmen – Rome's first flat-pack temple! This is another indicator of the huge influence on Rome of her conquest of the rich Greek areas of the Mediterranean.

The Temple survived by being converted into a church, Santo Stefano delle Carrozze (St Stephen of the Carriages, after the carriage workshops once nearby). Deconsecrated in the 19th century, it was left in isolation by Mussolini's demolition of the structures which had enveloped it in the Middle Ages.

In the middle of city and Tiber was the **TIBER ISLAND**, to the ancient Romans simply Insula (The Island). In reality a build-up of river silt, the Island arose according to legend in 509 BC with the expulsion of Tarquin, the last king. The people stormed his estate, cut down his corn, cursed it and threw it in the Tiber where, covered in mud, it became the island. In a grislier version, Tarquin lies below it.

THE RIVER TIBER

THE RIVER TIBER was in every sense at the heart of the ancient city. It was worshipped as a deity in its own right, and was also central to Rome's foundation legends in which the infants Romulus and Remus, abandoned on the river, were washed up at the foot of the Palatine Hill. The Tiber played a crucial role in Rome's history, as both a defensive barrier and, in times of peace, a major highway for goods and people. The navigability of the ancient Tiber and the presence of an important ford across the river both contributed to Rome's rise, though its frequent, devastating floods wreaked havoc until the 19th century.

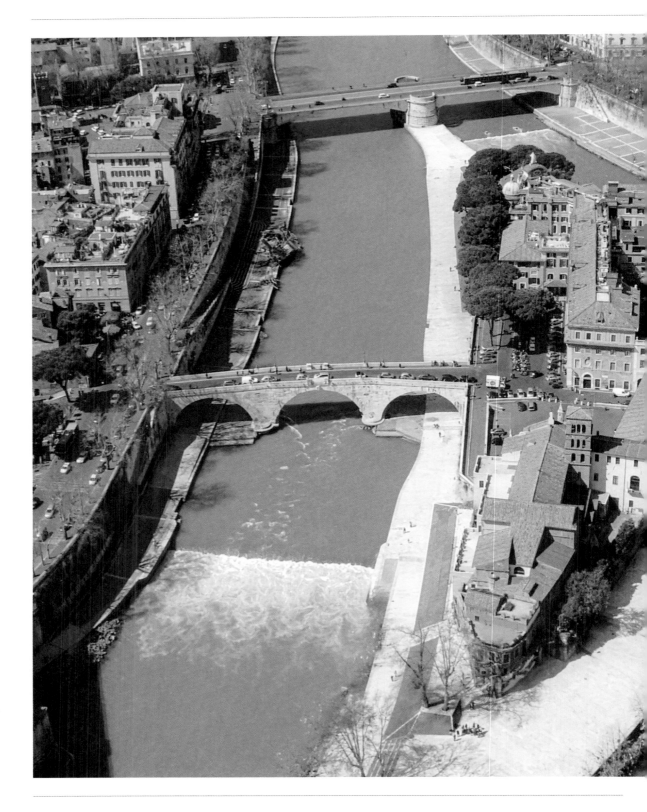

The Island was associated with health following a terrible plague in the 290s BC. Rome sent ambassadors to Epidaurus in Greece, the home of Asclepius, the god of healing. Their boat returned with a snake, the god's sacred animal, and when it neared the Island, the snake swam to it. A temple was built to the god, probably below the present church of San Bartolomeo (St Bartholomew), and the plague stopped. Because of this legend, and the island's boat-like shape, the Romans clad part of the Island in travertine to resemble a ship. Still just visible on the 'prow' is the head of Asclepius and his snake-entwined staff. People came to the temple to pray for good health, and its colonnades acted as a hospital; the Island still hosts a hospital today. When the riverbed was dredged in the 19th century, countless Roman terracotta votives were found, left by thousands of pilgrims over the centuries.

Linking the Island to the banks of the Tiber are two bridges. The **PONS CESTIUS**, built around 40 BC, was linked to the west bank and repaired in the AD 390s with stone from the portico of the Theatre of Marcellus: at the end of the Empire even major monuments were at risk of being quarried. The bridge was

Previous pages: Aerial view of the Tiber Island and the surrounding area. Of the seven Roman bridges that crossed the Tiber, three have survived, of which two link the Island to the city. The ancient Tiber, seen as a deity, was a major supply route, but in modern times has been massively embanked in order to prevent its disastrous floods.

Opposite: A reconstruction of the Tiber Island in around AD 100. The Island was sacred to Asclepius, god of healing, and his temple and its porticoes (which also functioned as hospitals) are clearly shown. The Island still hosts a church and a hospital today. The front of the island is fashioned into a boat, connected in legend to the god.

Right: The Pons Fabricius, linking the Tiber Island to the east bank, is the oldest surviving of Rome's seven bridges. Built in 62 BC by Lucius Fabricius – whose name is visible in the inscription here – the bridge survived the centuries because its design incorporates arched openings in its piers which reduce the pressure of flood water.

seriously damaged and reconstructed following the Tiber embankment works in the 1880s. The **PONS FABRICIUS**, linking to the east bank, is the oldest surviving bridge in Rome. Built by Lucius Fabricius in 62 BC to replace an earlier, wooden bridge, it is made of brick and concrete, originally faced with travertine. Inscriptions name Fabricius as 'CUR[ATOR] VIAR[UM]', that is, the superintendent of roads (and bridges).

Two four-headed pilasters with portraits of Janus set up at the end of the parapet give the bridge an alternative modern name of Ponte dei Quattro Capi. Yet another name is the Ponte dei Giudei, reflecting its proximity to the Jewish ghetto. This bridge, now lined with musicians, bag-sellers and artists, has survived more or less intact from the time of Julius Caesar. One of the main reasons for this is its clever engineering. The two main arches of the bridge are perfect semi-circles, providing maximum diffusion of any stress or thrust. In addition, the arched opening inserted into the central pier, together with two smaller openings at the ends (now built into the 19th-century embankments), served to channel flood water through and reduce the stress on the structure.

A growing city and its increasing traffic needed bridges. By the end of the Empire there were seven spanning the Tiber, of which three survive intact – the two island bridges and the Aelian Bridge to Hadrian's Mausoleum. Bridges not only took travellers from one side of the river to the other, but also from one world to another (and over a deity – the Tiber), so they were placed in the charge of priests. It is possible that the title *pontifex maximus*, given to Rome's supreme priest, derived from

Rome's Republican city walls, still over 8 m (26 ft) high, near Rome's main railway station. Confusingly called the Servian Walls (after Rome's sixth king Servius Tullius), they were built during the Republic in 390 BC. This photograph shows the interior of the wall, not originally visible under a great reinforcing earth bank or *agger*.

his power over these vital pathways. During the Empire the title was given to the emperor, and afterwards passed, as with so much imperial authority, to the popes.

Early Italy was a patchwork of independent, warring peoples, so cities needed strong defences, and Rome was no exception. The kings, perhaps Servius Tullius in the mid-6th century BC, first built walls around Rome. He had considerably extended the city and wanted it properly protected.

The later **REPUBLICAN CITY WALLS**, patchily visible today, were built in the 380s/370s BC in response to the catastrophic sack of Rome by the Celtic Senones tribe in 390 BC. They are called, confusingly, the Servian Walls, probably because they followed the original line. The circuit, over 11 km (almost 7 miles) long, enclosed 425 hectares (1,050 acres) in walls about 10 m (33 ft) high and 4 m (13 ft) wide and supported by an internal earth bank (*agger*). Some stones have masons' marks, in Greek letters, not Latin – showing either imported foreign expertise or the established presence of foreigners. The walls were well used until the Empire and its (relative) stability rendered them obsolete. They were then quarried for their stone, built over or incorporated into buildings, with *agger* particularly favoured for vineyards. The gates were often preserved as symbolic boundary markers and terminal points for Rome's roads.

Large stretches of the walls were uncovered during building works in the 19th and 20th centuries, and some parts remain above ground. The longest and best-preserved tract, about 9 m (29½ ft) high in places, is outside Rome's Stazione Termini, the main railway station; a smaller section is preserved in one of the station's McDonald's restaurants.

JULIUS CAESAR

(100–44 BC)

IN THE REPUBLIC'S last years, the 50s and 40s BC, one of the greatest figures was Gaius Julius Caesar, who made a profound impact on Rome and the world. Caesar was from the ancient Iulii family, descended in legend from the goddess Venus – a pedigree that was to prove a two-edged sword. Through military and diplomatic success and skilful manoeuvring, he made himself unopposed ruler of Rome. By 44 BC he had declared himself Dictator for life, revised the Roman calendar, and even brought his lover Cleopatra of Egypt to Rome.

In this period, Rome's architectural landscape had become ever more politicized. When the powerful general Pompey the Great (Julius Caesar's main rival) dedicated the first permanent theatre in Rome in 55 BC, he cleverly incorporated a Temple of Venus Victrix (Victorious Venus) at the top of the seating. This made the whole complex sacred – countering accusations of immorality and 'un-Romanness', which had dogged previous theatre projects – and also enabled the Senate to meet there. They assembled in the large hall at the back of the portico (now part of Largo Argentina), where Caesar would be murdered in 44 BC.

In order to eclipse Pompey's theatre, Caesar lined up a series of major building projects, to give him the monumental (in every sense) kudos he desired. These included his own theatre (finished as the Theatre of Marcellus by Augustus) and, in the Forum Romanum, a great basilica (Basilica Julia), the speakers' platforms (*rostra*) and a new Senate House (Curia). In addition he had plans to embank the Tiber (nineteen centuries before it actually happened), to stop its devastating floods. He did not live to see these projects realized. On the Ides (15) March 44 BC

CAESAR'S NEW FORUM NOT ONLY MET THE PRACTICAL NEED FOR EXTRA SPACE, BUT ALSO GLORIFIED FOREVER THE MAN WHO BUILT IT

Statue of Venus Genetrix, mother of the Roman nation – a copy of the cult image from the Temple in Caesar's Forum. In legend, Venus was an ancestor of Caesar, and his close association with the deity – through his construction of the Temple – reinforced this divine claim. Many Romans, however, feared delusions of grandeur and (for Romans, even worse) kingly ambition.

he was murdered by conspirators led by Marcus Junius Brutus. This launched the final, bloody decade of Rome's century of civil wars, and the ultimate end of the Republic.

Caesar's star project was his new forum: the **FORUM OF JULIUS CAESAR** and its **TEMPLE OF VENUS GENETRIX**. The Forum Romanum could no longer accommodate the massive and growing volume of the Roman world's financial, legal and social transactions. Increasing this capacity was essential, but construction work here, so near to the Capitoline Hill, required massive engineering and levelling works. In addition, the area was already densely packed with commercial and private buildings. Just acquiring the land was problematic, and it cost a fortune (a task entrusted to his friend, the orator and statesman Cicero). The total sum paid was astronomical, perhaps 100 million *sesterces* – enough to pay nine legions for a year. The cost was worth it for Caesar.

Caesar's Forum comprised a Temple of Venus in a great open piazza surrounded by airy double-colonnaded porticoes, for shelter and for business. This new forum, enclosed in its great curtain walls and with one single prominent temple, differed in design, function and decoration from the gloriously cluttered and openly accessible Forum Romanum. Yet a forum of any sort was a place of gathering, and gatherings could, of course, be made very political – useful in the polarized late Republic. So open spaces were very helpful – as were platforms from which to address the assembled crowd. Hence the Temple of Venus, like the Temple of Castor and Pollux in the Forum Romanum, included an open area at the front of its podium, where speakers could address the people below.

Monuments have political importance and Caesar's new Forum not only met the practical need for extra space, but also glorified forever the man who built it. Ironically, Caesar's Forum and Temple also contributed to the climate of fear and suspicion that led to his downfall. The Forum's great Temple of Venus Genetrix, 'Venus the founding Mother' of the Roman race, pledged to the goddess in 48 BC (before the battle of Pharsalus at which Caesar defeated Pompey), was begun in 46 BC and completed along with the Forum by Caesar's adoptive son and successor Augustus in 29 BC. Dedicating the temple to Venus appealed to unity and tradition – and promoted his own interests, as she was the mother of Aeneas and the grandmother of Aeneas's son Ascanius (or Iulus), Caesar's legendary ancestor.

As with Pompey's theatre, the Temple in Caesar's Forum changed the complex from public piazza to semi-sacred space

– dedicated to a deity explicitly linked to Caesar – and therefore
also a very politicized space. In addition, Caesar's new Curia was
planned to link directly to the Forum, as if almost an annex to it.

The interior of the Temple had two storeys of columns
supporting a vaulted ceiling, and was covered with marble
sculpture featuring Venus's son Cupid. The cult statue was
by Arcesilaus, one of the greatest sculptors of Caesar's time,
and the Temple was filled with treasures, some given by Caesar
himself. These included a breastplate studded with British
pearls – from his expedition to Britain in 55–54 BC – and
several cabinets of antique gems (Caesar was an avid collector).

There was also a gilded bronze statue of the Egyptian queen,
Cleopatra, dedicated by Augustus after his conquest of Egypt
in 30 BC. Cleopatra had lived in Rome between 46 and 44 BC
as Caesar's lover – they even had a child, Caesarion. In the
ancient world the consort of a queen could only be a king,
which alarmed those who feared that (the hugely popular)
Caesar intended to return Rome to a (traditionally despised)
hereditary monarchy, with an heir already in place.... This
might well have contributed to his assassination. Moreover,
on a great plinth in the piazza stood a colossal bronze statue
of Caesar on horseback, probably inspired by a Greek statue of
Alexander the Great. This gave Caesar's opponents even more
food for thought.

For many senators the last straw was when a number
of them went to meet Caesar while the Temple of Venus was
being built. They had gone there, ironically, to shower him with
honours, but found him with his throne placed at the centre
of the podium. This link between himself and Venus was not
lost on them and, worse still, Caesar did not stand when the
senators entered the Forum.

The Forum of Julius Caesar was a model for all later imperial
forums, which, with their temples and piazzas flanked by
colonnades, are seen as Roman features. Yet in Caesar's time
his Forum was something eastern, Greek and revolutionary.
Siting the temple on the centre of the rear wall was very Roman,
but the great equestrian statue and the sweeping colonnades
evoked the Greek Mediterranean. More than this, with its
open politicization, Caesar's Forum effectively challenged
the Forum Romanum's monopoly on authority.

Later building projects in adjacent areas meant the
Forum was rebuilt on several occasions, most notably when
Trajan created his Forum. He largely rebuilt the temple, added
more business space to the colonnades and, remembering

practicalities, built a great semi-circular public latrine – with its own heating system.

Excavations have exposed almost the full extent of the Forum, but the physical remains are very battered. The podium of the Temple carries three re-erected columns, while some elements of the colonnade and business areas survive, as do scraps of steps and flooring, with columns lying where they fell. In fact, Caesar's Forum is an interesting example of the processes of decay that affected many of Rome's monuments. By the AD 550s, because of the sharp decrease in population and activity, soil began to accumulate in the piazza, and bronze workshops were set up in the porticoes, almost certainly recycling ornaments and statuary. By the 9th century, peasants farmed vines and other crops among the ruins; most marble paving and wall veneers were removed and reused or burned for lime, while columns were reused in churches, or simply overthrown for their bases and capitals. By the 10th century the Forum was laid out with stone houses along purpose-built roads – a monument of ancient Roman civic order and power giving way to the new realities of medieval Rome.

The great red-brick **CURIA** (Senate House), the seat of Republican Rome's power, is one of the most complete structures in the Forum Romanum. The original Curia was burned down by rioters in 52 BC and this new Curia building was planned by Caesar and finished by Augustus in 29 BC. On the façade facing the Forum was a columned porch, with the rest of the exterior adorned with marble and stucco resembling masonry. Its great bronze doors were taken to the cathedral of San Giovanni in Laterano in the 1660s – those we see today are replacements. This Curia now adjoined Caesar's Forum, to which it was linked by two doors in its rear wall. The Senate would be in Caesar's shadow.

Rome's traditions had a strong element of conservatism, clearly visible in the Curia. Senators (about 300 in the Republic, rising to around 500 during the Empire) had no fixed seats but each sat on his stool of office (*sella curulis*), ranged on shallow tiered platforms. Neither was there a fixed heating system, and Cicero recalls how a meeting in 54 BC was called off because everyone was so cold (much to the amusement of the people outside). But in its remodelling after a fire in the AD 290s, its decor, at least, became more opulent. The floor was laid with intricate inlaid marble patterns (*opus sectile*), and much still survives. The walls had columned niches for statues,

THE NEW
CURIA NOW
ADJOINED
CAESAR'S
FORUM.
THE SENATE
WOULD BE IN
CAESAR'S
SHADOW

The Curia, seat of Rome's Senate, and, thanks to its conversion into the church of St Adrian, the best-preserved building in the Roman Forum. The holes on the façade once held rafters to support the original porch. Caesar was not assassinated here, but in the Senate's temporary meeting place near the Theatre of Pompey. Although Caesar planned this new Curia, it was only completed by Augustus after Caesar's death.

with the area above also in *opus sectile*, still visible in the 1560s. The ceiling, over 30 m (98 ft) high, was completely covered in gilding.

Against the far wall was the statue and altar of Victory, placed in the Curia by Augustus in 30 BC after he conquered Egypt. These were some of the most potent symbols of the power and traditions of pagan Rome, and provoked a war of wills between later Christian emperors and the old pagan elite. In AD 357 the statue was removed to Constantinople by the emperor Constans II. Put back by the pagan emperor Julian ('the Apostate') a few years later, it remained, even under Christian emperors, as a traditional, but not religious, element of Rome's glorious past, but the altar was removed permanently in 382. Around 630 the Curia became the church of St Adrian of Nicomedia, implying the Senate, last recorded as meeting in 603, either no longer existed or no longer warranted this grand building in the Forum. A cornerstone of the structure of society in ancient Rome had disappeared.

In front of the Curia was the **ROSTRA** or speakers' platform, so important to Rome's political life. This area of the Forum was associated with public assembly, law-giving and civic organization, so oratory was important, as was timekeeping. In the 260s/250s BC this area was the site of Rome's first public sundial, while the nearby Basilica Aemilia hosted another

Above: Detail of the Curia's remarkably well-preserved floor with intricate patterns of cut marble (*opus sectile*). This floor was laid in the early AD 300s during the rebuilding of the Curia after a disastrous fire.

Opposite: Reconstruction of the Curia in around AD 300. Senators, standing or seated on a backless ceremonial chair (*sella curulis*), debated and (less often) decided the direction of the Roman state. Real power lay with the emperor, who often presided personally over the Senate's activities.

timekeeping device, a public water clock (for days when, as happens even in Rome, the sun does not shine).

The platform was named after the metal prows (*rostra*) of warships captured in battle that were fixed into the platform as trophies. Caesar's Rostra, with its great curved, marble façade, saw many important public addresses, including a very risky sounding-out of public opinion by Caesar. Caesar, seated on a gilded chair, was offered a golden (royal) diadem by his then deputy Mark Antony. Polite clapping when Antony proffered it turned to riotous applause when Caesar ostentatiously refused it – a real warning, if only Caesar could have heeded it. A truly gruesome moment came in 43 BC when Mark Antony used the Rostra to display the severed head and hand of the orator Cicero, who had often attacked Antony in his speeches.

Augustus brought the frontage forward and created a great flat wall, complete with slots for the prows. On this new Rostra, Augustus's own body was displayed, not in the dismembered disgrace of Cicero, but on a gold and ivory couch, with imperial purple covers. The Rostra maintained its importance into the Empire, with 4th-century emperors such as Diocletian and Constantine embellishing and using it. Its importance gradually decreased as the old social structures, including the importance of public debate, passed away.

II.

FROM BRICK TO MARBLE

AUGUSTUS

(R. 27 BC–AD 14)

I N HIS WILL, Caesar named his great-nephew Octavian as his heir. Octavian defeated his adopted father's assassins and finally, in 31 BC, after numerous alliances of war and marriage had risen and fallen, and with his trusted deputy and future son-in-law Marcus Vipsanius Agrippa by his side, he defeated Mark Antony and Queen Cleopatra of Egypt at the sea battle of Actium. A year later, after their suicides, he seized Egypt, ending the civil wars which had plagued Rome for almost a century. Octavian was now the undisputed leader of the Roman world, and a grateful Senate showered him with honours and titles, including the very senior title of Augustus, 'the venerable/revered one', the name by which he was increasingly known. He immediately set about demonstrating his authority over the Roman world – a world that now could truly be called the Roman Empire.

Unsurprisingly, Rome was his major focus and, after decades of civil war, it needed attention. Augustus divided the city into fourteen regions, with organizations for religious and civic life, covering everything from festivals to food handouts. He boosted neighbourhood pride by building local shrines and sanctuaries, and took care of urban practicalities such as roads, water supplies and other amenities.

But buildings were his most visible achievement and lasting legacy. On pillars outside his Mausoleum and in other public places throughout the Empire, inscriptions were set up after Augustus's death, which laid out his *Res gestae*, the summary of his life's major achievements, including all the monuments he had built or rebuilt. Suetonius commented that what Augustus found in brick he left in marble, and indeed, beautiful and

SUETONIUS COMMENTED THAT WHAT AUGUSTUS FOUND IN BRICK HE LEFT IN MARBLE

imposing marble-covered structures of many different types
and functions mushroomed throughout the city as never before.
All these structures added to the complexity and beauty
of Augustus's Rome and, very importantly, to the glory of
Augustus himself, whether directly or through reference to
his illustrious human and divine ancestors.

In the Forum Romanum, at the heart of Rome, many
monuments took final form under Augustus, including the
great basilicas – Julia and Aemilia – and the new Curia, planned
by Julius Caesar. An important new monument, the Temple
of the Divine Julius Caesar, underlined Augustus's filial piety
and reminded people that Augustus's rule was validated by
Caesar, and his divine ancestor Venus. All monuments were
built with the approval of the emperor, but not all were his work.
In the Forum Romanum, the future emperor (and Augustus's
stepson) Tiberius remodelled the Temples of Concord and
of Castor and Pollux.

Forming the southern side of the Forum Romanum was the
BASILICA JULIA. Caesar had wished to replace an earlier basilica
here, on a much grander scale, using gold from his wars in France.

Completed by Augustus, it promptly burned down but the rebuilt basilica, dedicated in AD 12, kept the name of Caesar's family: Julia.

Roman basilicas were inspired by Greek prototypes, but the Roman version was different and much grander. The Basilica Julia was immense, measuring 105 × 60 m (344½ × 197 ft). Its aisle vaults, with their painted, gilded plasterwork, were 21 m (69 ft) high, while the gilded wooden ceiling floated at a dizzying 32 m (105 ft). The Basilica's decoration was sumptuous – façade, paving and wall veneer all of pure marble.

Some sense of the appearance of Roman basilicas can be gained from the large early churches of Rome, such as the 5th-century AD church of Santa Maria Maggiore, whose aisled form, high ceiling and gilded decoration, statuary and fine marble convey some of the atmosphere. Yet the Basilica Julia was longer, wider, taller and more graceful. From the outside, too, the Basilica was beautiful. Its sweeping arcades contributed to and enhanced the sense of theatre that characterized the Forum. The bustling terraces of the Basilica, facing onto the Forum piazza, were crammed with spectators jostling to see the imperial triumphs, processions and other events.

Much of the Basilica Julia was divided into 'courts', separated by curtains or screens, for use by magistrates called the *centumviri*, 'hundred men', who deliberated on wills and property, in sometimes highly controversial and dramatic cases. The public could watch from the galleries, and Pliny records a case he presented to a full house that was on tenterhooks, '*magna expectatio*'. He successfully defended a young noblewoman, Attia Viriola, disinherited by her eighty-year-old father in favour of his second wife. Pliny says he sailed through the speech on a sea of eloquence, dignity, anger and passion. Drama and oratory were clearly as important as legal knowledge – the word *actor* in Latin means a legal prosecutor/plaintiff as well as a theatrical performer.

Some spaces in the Basilica were used by bankers (*argentarii*) and moneylenders (*nummullarii*). One inscription commemorates a banker, Tiberius Flavius Genethlius, who formerly had a successful riding career. The emperor Caligula practised a different sort of money handling when he spent days throwing coins from the roof into the crowd below.

The Basilica Julia was gutted by fire several times, and after the major Forum Romanum fire of AD 283, the emperor Diocletian replaced the Basilica's graceful but weak columns with robust brick piers (marble-veneered, of course). In late

Previous pages: Reconstruction of the Basilica Julia in around AD 330. The Basilica closed the long southern side of the Forum Romanum, its arches and sculptures adding greatly to the Forum's splendour. Although the form and name (meaning 'royal hall') came from the Greek world, basilicas epitomized Roman urban landscapes from Rome to the provincial cities of Britain, such as Cirencester and York.

Opposite: Interior of the basilica church of Santa Maria Maggiore. There were differences in layout and function between the pagan Roman and early Christian basilica, but these early churches give us our closest idea of the interiors of the great basilicas of ancient Rome.

BASILICA

IN ANCIENT ROME a basilica was not a Christian church, but a building for business, court cases, legal administration and cultural gatherings. The Greek word *basilika* (kingly/royal), from *basileus* meaning a king, was often applied to porticoes or stoas: long two-storeyed covered colonnades, for commerce and law-giving in the city centres of the Greek Eastern Mediterranean. But the Roman version was grander, with a forest of columns creating four two-storeyed aisles around a central open nave. A mezzanine floor around the aisles created a gallery for watching proceedings within the building, or giving views to outside. Some basilicas had an apse for magistrates in legal cases.

Basilicas became ever more important as the financially complex, bureaucratic and litigious Roman world expanded. They were some of the largest and most conspicuous urban landmarks, and every major town had one, usually in the Forum. Rome naturally had several, concentrated in the Forum Romanum with its great long basilicas – Julia and Aemilia – closing the long sides of the Forum, and the immense Basilica of Maxentius dominating its east end.

From the 4th century AD Christianity adopted the form, slightly modified, with aisles down only the long sides, and the side entrance colonnade walled in to enclose the church space. This aisled, internally open form permitted a larger, less restricted gathering of believers, unnecessary in pagan temples where sacrifice and other rites took place outside the building at the altar. Churches were often modelled on Roman basilicas and, ironically, with their original inspiration long since vanished, these major Christian monuments are now the best way to glimpse the impact, scale and beauty of the great basilicas of ancient Rome.

antiquity the Basilica also served as an art gallery. In AD 415, five years after Alaric the Visigoth's sack of Rome, the urban prefect Probianus restored the Basilica, enhancing it with important sculptures including original works by famous Greek sculptors such as Polyclitus and Praxiteles.

As closed and disused pagan temples decayed, were vandalized or even dismantled, monuments such as the Basilica Julia became safe havens for these ever more vulnerable works. This was not in itself a pro-pagan act, but an attempt to sustain the idea of a cultured urban centre. Beautiful art, even though pagan, could still bring authority and validation to Christian Rome.

The Basilica became increasingly redundant and its size made it impossible to maintain. A small church was installed in the now ruined Basilica in the 7th/8th centuries AD, and workshops of *marmorarii* (marble workers) were set up, cannibalizing the decoration of the Basilica itself and covering its beautiful floor in heaps of marble chips. Most of the Basilica disappeared in the Renaissance, while 'excavations' in the 18th and 19th centuries took away the original marble floor and the church. Today, only reconstructed marble steps, a few brick piers and an expanse of pier stumps attest the importance of this beautiful building in Rome.

Just beyond the Curia, under the looming Capitoline Hill, was the splendid **TEMPLE OF CONCORDIA AUGUSTA**, the Temple of Augustan Concord (Harmony). It replaced a temple of the 120s BC, built by the Senate to mark the defeat and murder of the populist, reforming Gracchi brothers and many of their followers. On the eve of the dedication of the Temple, dissenters daubed on it, 'Concord has arisen from mad discord.'

It was rebuilt in AD 10, by Tiberius, who dedicated it, very diplomatically, to Concordia Augusta. The Temple had a plan that was radically different from others, in that it extended not frontally outwards, but sideways along the base of the Capitoline Hill to fill the space available. A columned porch led into a great rectangular *cella*, a museum and art gallery, filled by the imperial family with masterpieces of art and all illuminated by light from two great windows – another unusual feature. The quantity and quality of the artwork in the *cella* was exceptional. Niches contained masterpieces of sculpture by famous Greek artists; other works of art were given by Augustus himself, including paintings and a unique group of four elephants made of obsidian (volcanic glass). The pediment and roof were crammed with statues of Jupiter, Juno and Minerva as well as Mars, Venus, Peace and many others. In the AD 700s, the

Opposite: Reconstruction of the Temple of Concordia Augusta (Augustan Harmony), which was rebuilt by Tiberius to honour his adopted father Augustus. The Temple's great widthwise form was unique, as were the two great windows providing light for the *cella* and its museum-like collection of treasures. These included Greek paintings and sculptures and elephants carved from obsidian.

SPQR

EADEM CONCORDIAE VETVSTATE COLLAPSAM
IN MELIOREM FACIEM OPERE ET CVLTV SPLENDIDIORE RESTITVIT

Temple became a church welfare centre, and survived largely
intact until the 1450s, when it was razed for building materials.
Only the massive monolithic threshold of the *cella* is still *in situ*,
too much even for the Renaissance robbers.

Closing the short end of the main Forum area was the
TEMPLE OF DIVUS IULIUS, the Deified (Divine) Julius Caesar,
built by Augustus where Caesar's body was cremated after
his assassination. From Augustus onwards, this would
normally have taken place at a cremation precinct or *ustrinum*
in the Campus Martius, but the mob cremated Caesar here
in the heart of Rome, spurred on by Mark Antony's speech
from the Rostra. The remains were only partly burnt, and Cicero
bitterly lamented the rushed and botched cremation. To underline
his filial piety, Augustus built the Temple in the middle of the
Forum, in full view of those attending the Senate House – in

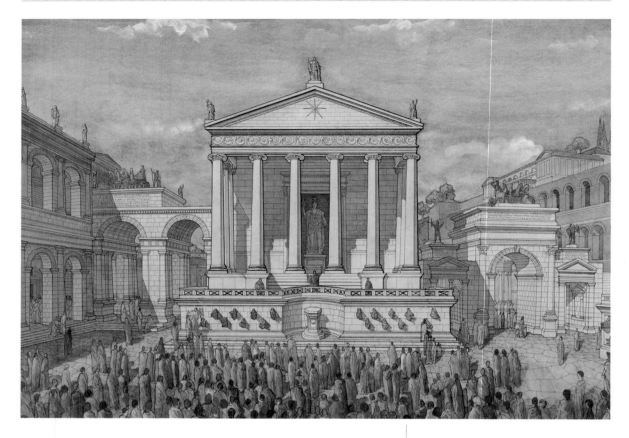

particular those who may have supported the assassins.
It was dedicated with great pomp in 29 BC, with weeks
of gladiator and beast fights, theatrical performances and
athletics, as a reminder that Augustus's rule was validated
by Caesar and therefore his divine ancestor, Venus.

The monument was revolutionary in that, in contrast to
the dozens of temples and shrines dedicated to deities across
the city, this one was dedicated to a man. After Caesar's death,
the Senate decreed that Caesar was *divus* – deified, so not a
god (*deus*), but very close. There was doubtless pressure from
Octavian and Caesar's other supporters, and the process was
helped by an incredible natural portent when a comet appeared
during games to mark his funeral in 44 BC. Known as the Julian
Star – *sidus Iulium* – it burned so brightly it was visible by day.
The heavens were reclaiming their own.

The Temple itself, set on a high podium in Roman style
(also useful against flooding) was not unusual. Uniquely, it had
a semi-circular recess in the podium for a circular altar marking
the exact spot where Caesar was cremated. Fresh flowers still

Opposite, above:
Reconstruction of the Temple
of Divus Iulius. A statue of
Caesar looks through the
doors, and the rostra is studded
with prows from Octavian's
(Augustus's) victory at Actium.

Opposite, below: Coin on which
Octavian is styled as *divi f(ilius)*
(son of a god), 36 BC. The
reverse of the coin shows the
Temple of Divus Iulius (*div. iul.*)
with the star (*sidus*) on its
pediment. Such coins were
powerful propaganda.

appear there every day. The front of the Temple formed
a new Rostra, studded with prows taken from the fleet of
Mark Antony and Queen Cleopatra at the battle of Actium
in 31 BC. This decisive sea battle became a huge part of
the narrative of Augustan rule. Inside, the main focus was
the cult statue of Caesar, with a star on his head – the comet
or 'Julian Star' seen after his death. Augustus filled the
Temple with precious objects, including a portrait of Venus
Anadyomene (Venus Rising) from the waves off Cyprus.
This famous painting by the renowned artist Apelles showed
Venus in the iconic pose of wringing out her hair, but sadly,
conservation was not a priority, and by the reign of Nero
in the AD 60s, around ninety years later, it had decayed so
badly it had to be replaced.

The Temple, though partly collapsed, survived until
the 1540s when it was completely levelled by papal contractors
seeking stone for the rebuilding of St Peter's. The rubble core
of the temple platform is, tragically, all that remains.

DEIFICATION

THE ROMAN EMPIRE was
full of gods, including the
deceased emperors
themselves. Becoming a
god after death – deification
(*consecratio*) – was borrowed
from Greek culture, like
many aspects of Roman life.
It became a major part of
imperial power, though
interestingly permission
to deify always came from
the Senate. It was a rare
opportunity for the Senate
to exercise its power (though
it seldom refused). Julius
Caesar was first to be deified,
followed by Augustus, then
many other emperors and
some other family members,
such as Livia, Augustus's wife.

If Caesar was *divus* (divine),
then Augustus, though still
alive, was *divi filius* (son of
the divine), hugely
strengthening his earthly
position. Deification spoke to
religion and statecraft – and
also architecture, because a
memorial temple was usually
dedicated to the new god.

At the funeral, attended
by tens of thousands, the
dead emperor's wax effigy
was displayed, usually on
a banqueting couch (though
Trajan's was driven around in
a chariot). After eulogies were
read, a huge procession took
the body to a cremation site
in the Campus Martius area,
north of the centre. It was

placed on a great, multi-
tiered funeral pyre, surrounded
by family and officials who
circled it several times before
lighting the fire, to much
choreographed mourning and
wailing. As fire consumed the
body, an eagle was released,
which soared upwards, carrying
the emperor's spirit up to
the gods. The Senate then
conferred *honores caelestes*
(heavenly honours), and the
emperor officially joined
the immortals. Not everyone
took the process literally and
seriously – Vespasian on his
deathbed said, 'oh heavens,
I think I'm becoming a god…'.

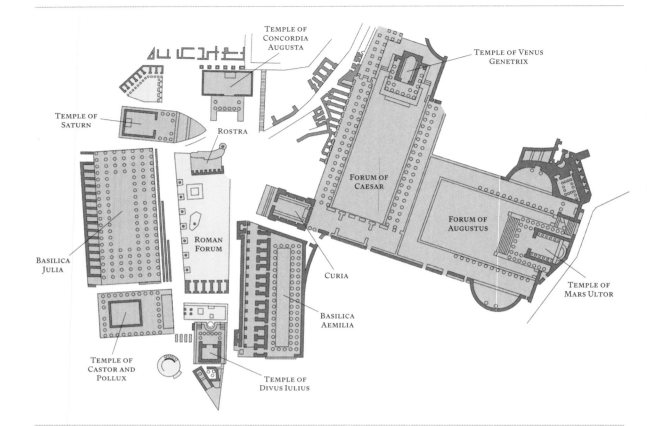

TEMPLE OF
CONCORDIA
AUGUSTA

TEMPLE OF VENUS
GENETRIX

TEMPLE OF
SATURN

ROSTRA

FORUM OF
CAESAR

FORUM OF
AUGUSTUS

ROMAN
FORUM

BASILICA
JULIA

CURIA

TEMPLE OF
MARS ULTOR

BASILICA
AEMILIA

TEMPLE OF
CASTOR AND
POLLUX

TEMPLE OF
DIVUS IULIUS

Augustus dutifully completed Julius Caesar's monumental projects, and set to work on his own **FORUM OF AUGUSTUS** and its **TEMPLE OF MARS ULTOR**. The Forum comprised a large open piazza surrounded by colonnades and the Temple of Mars Ultor. It provided extra capacity for the civic administration, primarily of law and (appropriately for a Forum linked to Mars) procedures connected with war. But the Forum also glorified the emperor, his reign and dynasty. It was filled with relevant imagery, including statues of himself and his family, while the Temple was a personal link between him and Julius Caesar, demonstrating the power of the regime. Yet even Augustus had problems acquiring the necessary real estate, hence the odd shape of one corner.

The main entrances were through gates in the massive firewall, 33 m (108 ft) high, which Augustus erected around his Forum to protect it from the frequent and disastrous fires that often originated in the Subura, a tenement slum area, north of the Forum. Later imperial forums also included firewalls, reinforcing the distinctive nature of each and remaining a major

A plan of the Roman Forum at the death of Augustus shows how every major structure was built or restored by him (in green). From the great basilicas and the Curia to the Rostra and temples both old (Saturn, Castor and Pollux) and new (the deified Julius Caesar) Augustus left an indelible mark. Nearby, rose the new Forums of Caesar and Augustus, both finished by him.

Below: A reconstruction of the interior of one of the side apses (*exedrae*) of Augustus's Forum. The innovative design provided spaces for legal matters and was lined with statues including one of Augustus's legendary ancestor the Trojan prince Aeneas (visible centre).

Overleaf: A reconstruction of the Temple of Mars Ultor, built of white marble with statues of bronze or painted marble. The piazza colonnades were filled with sculptures, while along the architrave were caryatids, and roundels of Jupiter Ammon, showing Augustus's dominance over Greece and Egypt. Over everything loomed the protective fire walls.

feature of the landscape into the Middle Ages. Augustus's firewall, made of grey-green tufa, with blocks and bands of white travertine, is pocked with holes for scaffolding, while ghosts of windows and doorways show reuse after the Empire.

The full impact of the Forum is lost, as so much of it is still below the nearby street, the Via dei Fori Imperiali (Road of the Imperial Forums). Originally it measured 125 × 118 m (410 × 387 ft), a vast expanse of white marble framed by long, two-storey colonnades. The second storey featured caryatids, pillars sculpted in the shape of women, copied from the Erechtheion on the Acropolis in Athens. These alternated with busts of Jupiter Ammon with his distinctive ram's horns, a favourite deity of Alexander the Great, the mighty conqueror. Visitors saw the Forum's unusual and beautiful decoration, and some understood its narrative: Rome's (Augustus's) conquest of Greece and Egypt and assumption of their wealth and authority. The walkways under the colonnades were covered with rare marble paving and veneer and filled with statues of marble, bronze, silver and even gold. Pliny placed it among the most beautiful monuments in the world.

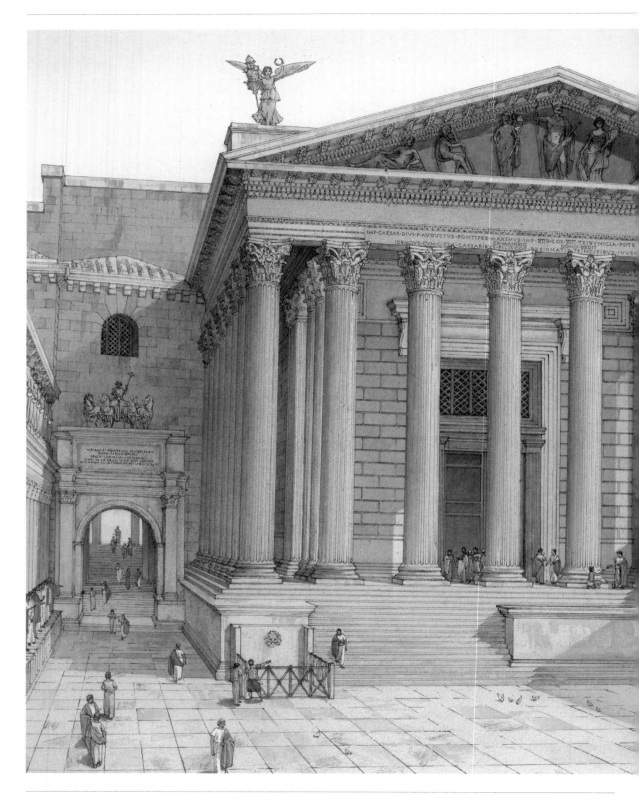

IMP·CAESAR·DIVI·F·AVGVSTVS·PONTIFEX·MAXIMVS·IMP·XIIII·COS·XIII·TRIBVNICIA·POTE
EX·MANIBIS·DICOQ·DEDIT
IDEMQVE·CVM·C·ETL·CAESARIB·FILIANDOS·RESIGNATIS·PRINCIPIBVS·IVVEN

Innovative, and later copied in Trajan's Forum, were great two-storey apses (*exedrae*) for legal proceedings, opening onto the square, and lined with statues of importance to Augustus. In the southern apse was a statue of Romulus, and the colonnade was filled with generals, statesmen and personifications of imperial provinces, underlining the reach of Rome's Empire. In the northern apse was the Trojan prince, Aeneas, son of Venus; his father Anchises, Venus's lover; and his son Ascanius (or Iulus, from whom Caesar's Julian family traced their lineage). The colonnade housed statues of their descendants, the Julio-Claudian imperial family, and at the end was a large room, dominated by a colossal statue of Augustus 12 m (over 39 ft) high. It stood against the far wall, which was painted blue and red with flowers and palmettes, like a great undulating curtain.

The centrepiece was the Temple of Mars Ultor (Mars the Avenger). Mars was the god of war and his temple commemo-rated the deaths of Brutus and Cassius, ringleaders of Caesar's assassination, at the battle of Philippi in Greece in 42 BC. The link between avenging god and avenging son was clear.

The Temple of Mars was, appropriately, the meeting place for the Senate when declaring war, and became the base of the Salii – the 'leaping' priests (named for their high-stepping ritual dance) who officiated at these ceremonies. Here generals sacrificed before leaving the city on campaign, and dedicated seized enemy standards. Mars was patron of males in general, so freeborn boys, on reaching puberty, dedicated their birth amulet or *bulla* to him.

The Temple, set on a high podium, had a sweeping staircase flanked by fountains, with the altar at the centre, while its massive pediment contained colossal statues of Mars, Venus and other deities. Deep diagonal lines in the firewall preserve the pitch of the towering temple roof. Its columns and walls were made of white Carrara marble, with the *cella* crusted with multicoloured marbles from Turkey and North Africa.

In the apse was a colossal statue of Mars, flanked by Venus and the deified Julius Caesar, underlining the divine origins of Caesar and Augustus. Around Mars were legionary standards, recaptured from Parthia (Iran). The Parthians had defeated Rome on several occasions, so their submission to Augustus was hugely significant. Other important dedications in the Temple included an ivory statue of Apollo and Julius Caesar's own sword. The Temple of Mars Ultor, like others such as Castor and Pollux, was also a security vault for Rome's wealthy citizens. Juvenal reports, however, that one night audacious (and

PLINY PLACED THE FORUM AMONG THE MOST BEAUTIFUL MONUMENTS IN THE WORLD

Opposite: Statue of Mars, god of war, in full military uniform. It is a copy, perhaps of the AD 110s–120s, almost certainly modelled on the cult statue in the Temple of Mars Ultor. Mars guided Rome's military successes and, as father of Romulus and Remus, was also present at the moment of its foundation.

Above: Bust of Octavia, sister of Augustus, only the second mortal woman to be commemorated in sculpture in Rome. Octavia was widely loved and respected; for many Romans, she was the epitome of dutiful and modest Roman womanhood.

sacrilegious) robbers broke in, stole the valuables and took Mars's gilded helmet for good measure. The Forum was also used for public prosecutions, and the emperor Claudius, presiding one day, almost quit the case because of the delicious smells coming from the kitchens of the Salians.

Until the 1930s this area, with the exception of the three remaining marble columns, looked very different. It was filled with medieval and Renaissance houses, convents and gardens, all swept away in the 1930s by the Via dell'Impero (Empire Road), now Via dei Fori Imperiali. These and more recent excavations have revealed much of the Forum.

Excavations in the 1990s showed that the Temple was already being dismantled for its marble by the AD 490s. In the Middle Ages, the podium was part occupied by the monastery of St Basil, and then the Knights of St John, whose headquarters in Rome are still built into the ruins of the Forum. Even the most beautiful and significant monuments were not immune from decay or deliberate demolition as Classical Rome passed away.

To the north and west of the traditional monumental centre stretched the large expanse of the Campus Martius (Field of Mars), so called because it was traditionally a parade and training ground for the army. Formerly a largely empty area outside the *pomerium* (city boundary), in the last century BC the Campus Martius became increasingly monumentalized. In the lower Campus, near the Capitoline, was the great Theatre of Marcellus, dedicated to the late son of Augustus's sister Octavia, and the Portico of Octavia herself, emphasizing that the imperial family was a team, all serving the Roman people and requiring public respect. The adjacent Temple of Apollo Sosianus showed the power of Augustus and his ability to bring old political enemies onside. The monumentalization and politicization of Rome's landscape were gaining pace.

In Republican temple precincts, such as Largo Argentina, the focus was on the deities. In the imperial period, temples could be part of a larger, more diverse complex. Perhaps the best example was the **PORTICO OF OCTAVIA**, Augustus's (Octavian's) sister. Their family was politically important, so marriage for Octavia was determined by politics more than love. Her first marriage had both – and produced three children including her beloved son Marcellus (a potential successor to Augustus). She resisted (respectfully) Caesar's demand that she divorce her husband and marry Pompey, but after her husband's death, she was obliged to marry Mark Antony. He abandoned her for Cleopatra. Augustus never forgave this personal and political slight, though Octavia dutifully raised her own and her husbands' children. Marcellus's death in 23 BC was a catastrophic blow for her and also for Augustus. Though retiring from public life, she was admired and adored by the people, and her death in 11 BC plunged Rome into deep mourning. Very significantly, Octavia was deified – the first woman to be so honoured – and her image appeared throughout the Empire on sculptures, coins and other media.

Originally built in the 140s BC by the general Quintus Caecilius Metellus (called Macedonicus after his conquest of Macedonia), the Portico was filled with works of art, including life-size bronze statues of Alexander the Great's generals, pillaged from the Macedonian city of Dion. All were displayed in his magnificent triumph through the city before being placed in the Portico. Art carried political messages – and power – so

Opposite: *Portico of Octavia in Rome* by Luigi Bazzani, 1869. The painting shows a large tenement block built right up to the Portico and fishmarket stalls in and around it. A church, Sant'Angelo in Pescheria (St Angelo of the Fishmarket), built in the Middle Ages still occupies part of the walled-in porch.

Right: The Portico of Octavia was one of the finest temple complexes in Rome. Today the medieval and later structures have been cleared, and excavations have revealed the original Roman ground level and the remains of part of the monument's colonnades. Reused masonry, including column drums, from Septimius Severus's restoration of the portico can be seen through the columns on the interior of the inner pediment.

Augustus kept Alexander's generals in his rebuild of 14 BC, adding Greek old master paintings, including one of Alexander. There was also a bronze statue of Cornelia, mother of the reformist Gracchi brothers, and renowned for her Roman female virtues. This statue of the mid-2nd century BC was very important as it was the first of a mortal woman to be set up in Rome. The statue of Octavia was the second.

Sculptures displayed in museums, lacking their original context, cannot always convey their intended messages or original impact. In the Portico of Octavia the context was stunning. Entering through an impressive central porch, largely preserved, people came into a beautiful, extensive piazza of 135 × 115 m (442 × 377 ft), surrounded by a perimeter wall with colonnades outside and in. This was obviously useful for those using the Portico, but also for the audience of the nearby Theatre of Marcellus. In the piazza were temples of Jupiter Stator (Jupiter the Sustainer), Rome's first recorded all-marble temple, and Juno Regina (Juno the Queen). These were famous for their 'swapped' decoration, that is, the feminine appearance of the paintings and other decor in Jupiter's Temple and the masculine tone in the Temple of Juno. Pliny said this swap, though an error by the workmen, was taken as the gods' will and made permanent.

The Portico also contained two libraries, one of which housed works in Greek, and a Curia, used occasionally by the

Senate. The Portico was an important amenity for worshipping, deliberating, learning, mingling in the piazza, and admiring the artworks. This concept became popular in the Augustan period – though the Portico of Octavia was one of the first and most important. Far from simply a religious centre, the Portico and others like it were essential points of diffusion for the new Augustan Roman (or Greco-Roman) culture.

The complex perished in a conflagration in AD 80, and again in several others, but was definitively rebuilt by Septimius Severus in about AD 200. The inscription on the pediment tells how the Portico was 'INCENDIO CONSUMPTUM' (destroyed by fire). It also highlights Severus's name and titles and those of his elder son Caracalla (the essential visible acknowledgment of the generosity of the emperor). The main entrance porch, though considerably altered, still stands. Severus's rebuilding is evident on the interior of the pediment, clearly composed of *spolia*, or reused masonry, from structures damaged in the fire. This was never visible, but hidden by the coffered ceiling.

The great brick arch dates to the Middle Ages when it was part of the church of Sant'Angelo in Pescheria (St Angelo of the Fishmarket). The market was still held in and around the porch in the 19th century. The area around the Portico and Theatre has also been, from the 1550s, the Jewish ghetto. The Jewish community, present in Rome from the 1st century BC despite the discrimination and cruelty of the Renaissance and early modern periods and the horrors of the Second World War, is still based in this area.

Sadly, the libraries have disappeared and the temples were so thoroughly ransacked in the 1300s that only a column of the Temple of Juno survives, englobed in later buildings. But the shops, church and restaurants flanking the porch preserve the line of the perimeter wall, with several columns surviving from the colonnaded frontage. A trip downstairs in one or two of the restaurants brings you face to face with Roman masonry and columns.

Recent excavations revealed the original Roman ground level some 4–5 m (13–16 ft) below today's streets. Walking towards the Theatre of Marcellus, you see traces of original paving, columns and, over to the far right, a corner entrance to the Portico, flanked by grey granite columns, with some decorative marble still in place, hints of the monument's vanished splendour.

Right next to the end of the Portico is the **THEATRE OF MARCELLUS.** Existing buildings had to be demolished

Opposite: View by Giovanni Battista Piranesi of the Theatre of Marcellus, *c.* 1757, surrounded by houses, shops and churches. Once the 'Theatre Royal' of ancient Rome, its upper floor contained the palace of the Orsini, one of Rome's noble families, the middle floor its cellars and store rooms, and the lower storey – half interred – a mass of shops and workshops. These shops and the houses, piazzas and churches around were all swept away in the 1930s.

Overleaf: A view of the Theatre of Marcellus today. The upper floor still contains fine apartments (some for hire), while the first two storeys, preserving much of the Roman arcading, were emptied and restored in the 1920s–30s. The three white columns to the right are the re-erected remains of the Temple of Apollo Sosianus. They were discovered during works around the Theatre together with a group of original Greek sculptures that once decorated the pediment.

to construct it, including temples to Diana and Piety. The Theatre of Marcellus, together with Pompey's Theatre and the Theatre of Balbus, created a 'theatreland' in this part of Rome. The passage of theatregoers and the industry for feeding and watering them transformed surrounding areas. The noise of the audiences – around 20,000 people at Marcellus, 18,000 at Pompey and 12,000 at Balbus – amplified by the buildings, was incredible. Marcellus was the largest of these and is the only one to survive above ground. Caesar planned it to equal the theatre of his bitter rival Pompey, intending to build it in Greek fashion against a hill (Jupiter's hill, the Capitoline). By Caesar's death work had begun on this site, to be completed by Augustus.

The exterior had three storeys, as on the later Colosseum, in three Roman architectural styles – Doric on the first level, Ionic on the second and Corinthian on the third. The two lower storeys remain, the third displaced by the Renaissance apartments still there today. Sandwiched between stage and river were (quite small) colonnades and halls to shelter theatregoers, but the extensive Portico of Octavia was next door. Marcellus, like the Colosseum, had a canvas awning (*velarium*), to protect people from the elements.

Augustus inaugurated the Theatre in 11 BC, with theatrical performances and varied entertainments such as the first display in Rome of a tiger. Marcellus instantly became the most important in Rome – a 'Theatre Royal', in effect – and retained imperial favour. Vespasian rebuilt the stage and gave huge sums of money to the principal actors at the reinauguration.

The Theatre was used into the 5th century – as late as AD 421 a prefect set up statues on the stage. But even the Theatre Royal felt the changes, and by the 390s its porticoes were being quarried to repair a nearby bridge, the Pons Cestius. Turned into a fortress in the Middle Ages, from the early 16th century the Theatre was converted into apartments for

MUSSOLINI AND THE 'LIBERATION' OF ANCIENT ROME

AT THE BEGINNING of the 20th century, Rome's medieval, Renaissance and Baroque centre was still intact, but not for much longer. In the 1920s and 1930s, Italy's Fascist leader Mussolini resolved to uncover ancient Rome – the Rome of Augustus, the emperor with whom Mussolini associated himself so closely.

In 1922 he spoke of the need to 'liberate all of ancient Rome from its mediocre disfigurements'. So, through campaigns of mass demolition, Augustus's monuments including his Mausoleum, Forum and Temple of Mars, the Theatre of Marcellus and the Ara Pacis were all 'liberated'. Structures over and around them were swept away at lightning speed, as

Mussolini prepared Rome for the bi-millennium of Augustus's birth in 1937. Mussolini symbolically began the works himself, by wielding a pickaxe that smashed into the rooftiles of those doomed buildings.

Sometimes Mussolini's primary aim was not to expose ancient structures, but to improve infrastructure, especially roads. He built the Via dell'Impero, now Via dei Fori Imperiali, over the imperial forums as a triumphal road and parade ground, linking the Colosseum with his headquarters in Piazza Venezia. In doing so he razed a densely populated, intact Renaissance suburb to the ground, and displaced over 4,000 people. Many Roman monuments, it is true, are

only visible today thanks to Mussolini's 'liberations', but the devastation he caused to Rome's later architecture was incalculable. Fortunately for Rome's heritage, war meant that from 1941 Mussolini's pickaxe swung no more.

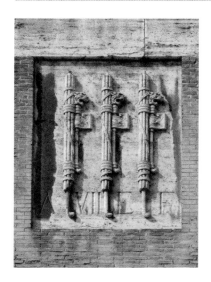

Panel on the Theatre of Marcellus, showing the *fasces* (an axe bundled with rods). The *fasces* was the symbol of ancient Rome's senior officials and was adopted by (and gave its name to) Mussolini's Fascist party. Mussolini added this panel when he constructed a supporting buttress in 1929 (or VII E.F., 'Era Fascista', the new Fascist age), as recorded here.

the Orsini and other noble families which, according to the 19th-century Prussian ambassador, Barthold Niebuhr, had gardens filled with fountains, flowers, orange trees and jasmine.

In the 1920s, the medieval quarter around the Theatre was torn down to make way for the new road to Ostia, the Via del Mare. As for the Theatre, the lowest level of arches had for centuries been filled with shops, taverns and storerooms. All were swept away, and soil and rubble (and metres of archaeology) were removed down to Roman paving, now poor and patched, but originally a gleaming apron of white slabs. Today the great, arched travertine exterior stands solid, though with holes in the façade showing the activity of salvagers, looking for metal masonry clamps. On the arches the first 2 m (6½ ft) of the stone are in very good condition, showing the height to which they were buried. The green tufa stone arches representing the outer façade are reconstructed, but the arches of brown tufa are the original interior, exposed where the original travertine façade is missing.

When Augustus dedicated the Theatre, he would have placed inscriptions on the building exalting Marcellus, but these have not survived. Mussolini, when he constructed a great supporting buttress, set into it a large commemorative tablet showing three *fasces* (the symbol of Mussolini's regime, borrowed from ancient Rome, comprising a bundle of rods round an axe), and a date according to the new Fascist calendar, 'A VII E.F.' ('Anno settimo dell'Era Fascista', that is, the seventh year of the Fascist Era, from Mussolini's march on Rome in 1922, so: 1929). For dictators and emperors alike, constructing or repairing buildings was a great way to show people their power and their generosity.

Almost touching the Theatre was the **TEMPLE OF APOLLO MEDICUS SOSIANUS**, first dedicated in the 430s BC to the Greek god Apollo as 'Medicus' (the healer), after plague ravaged Rome. It became, alongside the adjacent temple of the war goddess Bellona, a regular meeting place for the Senate when considering war, treaties and the awarding of triumphs.

In the 30s BC Gaius Sosius, a successful general, proposed a complete rebuild of the Temple. He had played an important role in Rome's provinces, especially Judaea (approximately modern Israel and Palestine), and was awarded a triumph for defeating rebels there and for putting Herod (of biblical fame) on the throne. He also campaigned in Rome's civil wars – but against Octavian – and even commanded part of Antony and Cleopatra's fleet at the battle of Actium. Octavian, now Augustus, surprisingly pardoned Sosius, who regained public office and was

Left: Fragment of a frieze that once decorated the interior of the Temple of Apollo Medicus Sosianus. The Temple was closely involved with matters concerning war and treaties. This decoration shows part of the triumph that marked the end of a successful campaign. Two bound prisoners sit dejectedly on a parade float (*ferculum*), while a trophy of captured shields stands over them.

Opposite: The Mausoleum of Augustus today, stripped of its decoration and veneer, leaving just brick and concrete. The gate, flanked by pillars bearing the *Res gestae* – Augustus's achievements – had a line of sight to the doors of the Pantheon.

allowed to complete his rebuilding of the Temple of Apollo. It was dedicated by Augustus on his own birthday, 23 September, but remarkably it still bore Sosius's name. Offering a building that embellished Augustan Rome was so important that it could smooth over major political differences. The more buildings Rome could vaunt (as long as Augustus approved), the better.

The scale of the Temple's three re-erected columns still impresses today, but Sosius's colonnade originally towered more than 20 m (65½ ft) above the people below. This densely built-up area became even more so with the Theatre; in fact the Temple lost its frontal staircase and was accessed only from the sides. The *cella* was crusted in rare marble from North Africa and the Greek islands and sumptuously decorated with paintings, statues and a frieze showing scenes from a triumph, reflecting the Temple's role in war. There was also an ancient cedarwood statue of Apollo from Lebanon and the famous statues of the 'Niobids'. These 5th-century BC Greek originals showed the slaughter of the children of Niobe, who boasted her fourteen children made her more important than Leto, the mother of only two – the deities Apollo and Artemis (Diana). Sadly the gods heard her hubris (arrogant pride) and killed her children in a blizzard of arrows.

The Temple's pediment showed Greek gods and heroes such as Athena and Theseus, legendary king of Athens, battling with the female warriors, the Amazons. Incredibly many of the sculptures were discovered in the 1930s, lying in

'THE MAUSOLEUM TELLS US TO LIVE, IT TEACHES US THAT THE GODS THEMSELVES CAN DIE'

MARTIAL

front of the Temple – a very rare survival of a group of original Greek sculpture. They date from the 5th century BC and are made of fine, Parian marble, once brightly painted, with attachments such as weapons in gilded bronze. They represent a tiny proportion of the original sculptures. Wealthy Romans were bringing ever more plundered art into the city.

All Augustan buildings glorified the emperor, but in the northern Campus Martius were two monuments of pure dynastic propaganda. Augustus's Mausoleum towered over the area, while the smaller, though equally symbolic, Ara Pacis (Altar of Peace) celebrated Augustus as bringer of peace and prosperity. In the rest of the Campus Martius, this monumentalization, begun by Augustus, was greatly advanced by his deputy and son-in-law Marcus Agrippa. Agrippa built a great complex of structures, including his public Baths (the first in Rome), a basilica and the first Pantheon. Rome needed more facilities and therefore more monuments, and the Augustan builders were very willing to oblige.

The **MAUSOLEUM OF AUGUSTUS** in the vast modern Piazza Augusto Imperatore is, together with the Ara Pacis Augustae, key to understanding Augustus's urban programme and his regime.

Opposite: Reconstruction of the Mausoleum of Augustus, with the lower rotunda planted with a lawn and cypress trees (though it's possible that the roof was simply domed). Completed by Augustus in his lifetime, it was the greatest of Rome's tombs, and was a revolution, both in size and design.

Below: Marble name blocks identified the resting places of the emperors and their family members. This block is inscribed for Agrippina (the Elder), Agrippa's daughter, Augustus's granddaughter and mother of the future emperor Caligula. Although she made an enemy of the emperor Tiberius and died in exile she was still buried in imperial style.

It was built by Augustus himself in 28 BC (over forty years before his death) for himself and his dynasty. Those buried in the Mausoleum included Augustus's sister Octavia, her son Marcellus (the first to be buried here), Augustus's wife Livia, his son-in-law Agrippa, and the later emperors Tiberius and Claudius.

Expressly barred were Julia (the Elder), Augustus's daughter, and Julia (the Younger), his granddaughter, both guilty of infringing (some said spectacularly) Augustus's new laws on adultery, part of his 'back to basics' moral programme. The monument was closed in AD 98 with the burial of the emperor Nerva. For the next century, emperors and family members (with the exception of Trajan, who was buried in a chamber at the base of his column) found rest in the Mausoleum of Hadrian.

The Mausoleum of Augustus was perhaps inspired by Etruscan round 'tumulus' tombs, or (more likely) by grand Greek tombs from the Eastern Mediterranean. The Mausoleum comprised concentric walls of tufa, brick and concrete forming two major drums. The outer wall was 87 m (over 285 ft) across, the largest in the Roman world, and was veneered in dazzling travertine limestone. The inner rose over 30 m (98 ft) high and, decorated with Doric columns, was topped by a great bronze statue of Augustus. Concrete vaults supported the roof, topped with either a smooth masonry dome, or a garden with trees and shrubs. At the entrance were bronze pillars recording the achievements of the deified Augustus – the *Res gestae divi Augusti* – and, added later, two Egyptian obelisks of red Aswan granite. All around was a beautiful park with trees and water features.

At the centre of the Mausoleum is a rotunda, the burial chamber itself, with niches containing great marble blocks, hollowed out to hold the precious ash urns of the dead. Accompanying them were marble name plaques, now nearly all lost. One survives for 'Octavia *soror*' (Augustus's sister) and another for 'Marcellus *gener*' (his nephew). One urn block belonging to Agrippina the Elder, Augustus's granddaughter and mother of the future emperor Caligula, was used in the Middle Ages as a grain measure. At least this preserved it. At the heart of the rotunda was a small, squared chamber for the remains of Augustus himself.

Some original paving remains visible in front of the Mausoleum. On part of it, archaeologists found diagonal and horizontal lines, almost certainly the blueprint for part of the pediment of the Hadrianic Pantheon. Exactly one-half of the pediment is represented, at full scale. Materials were perhaps being unloaded at the nearby river port, then 'mocked

up' prior to construction. It seems likely this diagram was intended to remain visible – a conscious link between Hadrian and his illustrious predecessor. Between the Mausoleum and Pantheon there had always been a strong link, and in fact, before the Campus Martius became built up, there was a perfect line of sight between the doorway of the Pantheon and the entrance of the tomb. Augustus's large, shining tomb dominated the Campus Martius – an extremely powerful dynastic statement. The poet Martial, noting a more subliminal effect of the monument, said, 'The Mausoleum tells us to live; that building nearby, it teaches us that the gods themselves can die'.

In the Middle Ages the Colonna family converted the Mausoleum into a fortress. This was dismantled in the 1160s, when much of the masonry and decorative marble were stripped

Detail of Palazzo Nord, one of the Fascist-period buildings erected around the Mausoleum. Mosaics illustrate the birth of Rome: a seated she-wolf, Romulus and Remus shown in a boat cradled by a personification of the River Tiber, and above him Neptune, god of the sea. Figures on the sides portray good honest labour – a favourite propaganda image of the regime.

'THE DEAD, BUT SCEPTRED SOVEREIGNS, WHO STILL RULE OUR SPIRITS FROM THEIR URNS'

LORD BYRON

Overleaf: The southern (front) side of the Ara Pacis, built to commemorate the establishment of peace by Augustus after his return from campaigns in Spain. It shows mythical figures from Rome's history: Mars with Romulus and Remus (left) and Aeneas (right) all linked genealogically with the emperor. Everything is brought together in typically ornate classical Augustan style.

away. Formal gardens occupied the ruins, followed in the 17th century by a wooden arena, used for bullfights and buffalo hunts. In the late 19th century a concert hall, the 'Auditorium Augusteo', was built inside the tomb, but was demolished in the mid-1930s to expose the Mausoleum.

In order to isolate and suitably frame the Mausoleum, Mussolini demolished many buildings, creating the large, austere Piazza Augusto Imperatore. The monument was framed by three new long buildings decorated with mosaics, inscriptions and sculpted friezes, showing themes and images typical of the Fascist period, from idealized and heavily gender-stereotyped citizens, to images of warfare – ancient and modern – and the legendary origins of Rome. On one building an inscription, flanked by *fasces*-carrying winged Victories, mentions the spirit of Augustus and praises Mussolini *dux* (the leader) for liberating the Mausoleum from the encumbrance of the centuries and for reassembling the Ara Pacis.

The Mausoleum's veneer is gone today, and the interior has bare walls and chunks of fallen vaulting, interspersed with battered fragments of decoration and inscriptions. Nevertheless, the structure has been conserved and can be visited. Though very ruined, the monument still has great power with, in Lord Byron's words, 'The dead, but sceptred sovereigns, who still rule our spirits from their urns…'. Mussolini was doubtless as affected as we are today by Byron's evocation. Were Mussolini's intentions purely to revere and celebrate Augustus? Or was the Mausoleum also intended to be the tomb of the self-styled new Augustus, Mussolini?

On the Tiber side of Piazza Augusto Imperatore, and framed now in a controversial, ultra-modern structure, is the reconstructed **ARA PACIS AUGUSTAE** (the Altar of Augustan Peace). Dedicated in 9 BC – on the empress Livia's fiftieth birthday – it marked the return of Augustus from military campaigns in Spain and France and celebrated the establishment of *pax*, Peace. The Romans worshipped Peace and other abstract concepts as a deity, so the altar was also a shrine to the goddess. It was originally built next to the main north–south road, the Via Lata (now Via del Corso), by which Augustus had returned to Rome, and it was near the Corso that parts of the altar first emerged in the 1560s. Other pieces were found in the mid- to late 19th century, when excavation stopped because of flooding and subsidence. Full excavation was ordered in 1937, and to protect the excavations from flooding, the surrounding earth was frozen. Many new pieces were retrieved, casts were taken of existing

Left: Panel from the northern (back) side of the altar screen, showing either a goddess – perhaps Pax (Peace) or Tellus (Mother Earth) – or a more allegorical figure such as Plenty. She is surrounded by peacefully grazing animals, contented children and deities of air and water, symbolizing the benefits of Roman Peace – the Peace that only Augustus was able to bring about.

fragments, and the altar was resited here on a tall platform. On the side facing the Mausoleum was inscribed in 15,000 bronze letters the text, originally set on bronze pillars by his tomb, of the *Res gestae divi Augusti* (Achievements of the Divine Augustus).

The altar was not relocated to Piazza Augusto Imperatore by chance, since both the Ara Pacis and Mausoleum projects were intended as part of the celebrations to mark the bi-millennium of Augustus's birth in 1937, overseen, of course, by Mussolini. The propaganda inherent in the Mausoleum and Ara Pacis in antiquity was still very relevant in the 1930s. The monument's focus was the central altar, at which officials and priests, including the Vestal Virgins, made a yearly sacrifice. But the most striking feature was the great marble curtain screen. Its interior was elegantly plain, with simple vertical panels below a band of Greek-style palmettes, and in the upper part sacrificial garlands of oak, myrtle and pine, between *bucrania* (stylized ox-skulls).

The exterior, on the other hand, carries some of the finest and most iconic of Augustan art. Like the inside, it was divided into two horizontal zones by a fine border. The lower zone was filled with luxuriant floral decoration, broken by entrances on the north and south sides but uninterrupted on the west (river) and east (Mausoleum) sides. It presented great tapestries of abundant, brightly painted plant life. Most prominent was acanthus, the most popular motif in Augustan art, with thick, torch-like stems carrying leaves and flowers all over the panels.

Below: Part of the frieze on the upper part of the east and west sides of the screen showing a great procession – perhaps the inauguration of the Ara Pacis. The two main figures are Augustus at far left and his son-in-law and deputy Marcus Agrippa in the centre. They stand out for their height, but also they are both shown with their heads covered, *capite velato*, ready to lead sacrifice.

Intertwined were other plants including thistle, laurel, vines, ivy, teasel and artichoke, and flowers from anemones to lilies and carnations. Wildlife included birds, frogs, lizards, scorpions and snails. On the west side, near the base of the acanthus, is a flash of dark humour, as a nest of chicks is menaced by a snake – and one makes a desperate dash for safety.

The upper level of the screen featured people and gods. People were, after all, above nature. Flanking the openings were scenes from Rome's legendary past. Front left, the god Mars watches shepherds discover his sons Romulus and Remus, being suckled by the she-wolf. Right is the Trojan prince Aeneas, the refugee from Troy and legendary ancestor of Romulus and Remus, who led his people to Italy. He is shown *capite velato*, head covered by his toga, sacrificing to mark the founding of his new kingdom.

At back right a badly damaged panel shows Dea Roma – the personification of the city. Back left, beautifully preserved, is one of the finest surviving examples of Augustan art: a seated goddess, perhaps Pax or Tellus (goddess of the earth), with children and flanked by other deities, riding on a *ketos* (sea monster) and a swan, representing air and sea. Cattle rest and sheep graze, while corn and acanthus spring from the rocks. Abundance and prosperity – the rewards of *pax Romana*.

Most important, then as now, is the procession on the long sides, possibly showing the dedication of the monument itself. In high and low relief, with realistic and dynamic change of pace, the procession features a 'who's who' of the imperial family, high-ranking statesmen and religious figures. Some seem clearly recognizable, but academics have argued over identifications for centuries.

The west side is less well preserved and shows the second half of the procession. Some people are carrying sacred jugs used for sacrifice or laurel leaves sacred to Apollo, Augustus's patron deity. Members of the imperial family, including children, process with senior magistrates, and at the front is a *lictor*, an attendant who carried the *fasces*, the symbol of authority of Rome's highest officials, including the two annually elected consuls, the most senior state figures after the emperor. The *fasces*, rods and axe, represented corporal and capital punishment.

The long east side facing the Mausoleum of Augustus is the procession's climax. Towards the rear are more of the imperial family – including Augustus's wife Livia and his daughter Julia (before she fell from favour), and imperial children wearing the *bulla*, a round amulet worn by boys until puberty. At the front more officials carry *fasces*, followed by senior priests – including *flamines* (with distinctive spiked caps). Most conspicuous is Augustus himself, and, soon afterwards, facing almost full-square onto us, Marcus Agrippa. They have their heads veiled (*capite velato*), and as important people they are also shown slightly taller than everyone else – a common convention in Roman art. This monument, while not Augustus's largest or grandest, encapsulates an important strand of his propaganda – Augustus the conqueror transformed into Augustus the bringer of peace.

Not all tombs were as grand as Augustus's, nor were they all circular. In the south of the city is the **Pyramid of Gaius Cestius**. Its inscriptions record that Gaius Cestius was an *epulo*, an official responsible for state religious feasts, and that the monument was constructed in 330 days. Built around 18–12 BC, it measures approximately 36 m (118 ft) high and 30 m (nearly 98½ ft) wide at the base. It is made of brick and concrete, with a well-preserved facing of white marble from Carrara in northern Italy. Inside is a vaulted burial chamber, with simple but elegant wall paintings. Four columns stood at the corners of the Pyramid, and two inscribed statue bases were discovered nearby in the 16th century, with fragments of their bronze statues.

Fascinatingly, the inscriptions tell us the statues were paid for by selling *attalici* – fine, expensive tapestries from the Greek

EGYPTOMANIA SWEPT THROUGH ROMAN ART AND CULTURE AFTER ROME'S CONQUEST OF EGYPT

Opposite: An inscription on the east face of the Pyramid of Gaius Cestius. This tomb was a great social statement, a reminder of Cestius's achievements, wealth and culture. This inscription records his role as a *septemvir epulonum*, a member of an elite college of priests who organised Rome's most important religious banquets.

city of Pergamon. Cestius hoped to take them with him to his grave, but Augustus's anti-luxury legislation prevented it. Clearly there was still money left over, as the inscription names Agrippa as one of Cestius's heirs. Currying favour with the imperial family by leaving them money was a good move for the surviving family. The monument survived because in the 3rd century AD it was built into the city wall. It was known in the Middle Ages as the 'Tomb of Remus', brother of Romulus, who himself was supposedly buried in another, larger pyramid sadly destroyed in the Renaissance, near the Castel Sant'Angelo.

These pyramids are part of the 'Egyptomania' that swept through Roman art and culture after Rome's conquest of Egypt, with Egyptianized monuments, Egyptian gods, and Egyptian imagery in mosaics, wall painting, jewelry and even tableware. At this time Augustus brought back great obelisks from Egypt to decorate public monuments such as the Circus Maximus and his Mausoleum; Egyptomania was fuelled still further.

The English writer Thomas Hardy was not impressed with Cestius's Pyramid, saying, 'Who, then, was Cestius, And what is he to me?...a man who died and was interred To leave a pyramid...'. and concluding the Pyramid served only one purpose – to indicate the tombs of Keats and Shelley in the nearby Protestant Cemetery.

Overleaf: The Pyramid of Gaius Cestius was originally free standing – its gleaming statues and marble facing designed to impress all those who arrived in Rome from Ostia. In the AD 270s the monument was incorporated into Aurelian's great wall circuit, which ensured its survival.

AUGUSTUS'S SUCCESSORS

A FTER THE REIGN of Augustus, with its abundance of fine monuments, the building record of his three immediate successors paled by comparison. The next emperor was Augustus's stepson, Livia's son Tiberius – not Augustus's first choice, of which Tiberius was constantly reminded. He was popular with the army and a good general and administrator. He erected some fine buildings in the Forum Romanum – the Temples of Castor and Pollux and of Concordia Augusta – but both were built before he was emperor and so their glory shone on Augustus. Tiberius was a reclusive character and spent long stretches in self-imposed exile in his Villa Iovis on Capri, which, though spectacular, had little impact in Rome. His last years were defined by paranoia and excesses, and terrible relations with the Senate. When he died in AD 37, his great-nephew Gaius (Caligula) took power. Hopes that this prince – so beloved of the army when he was young – might return Rome to the wholesome days of Augustus were soon dashed. Caligula suffered from delusions of grandeur (and divinity), was much too intimately close to his sisters, and descended into paranoia and violence. As for monuments, Caligula focused on vanity or pure pleasure projects such as the palace barges of Lake Nemi or the bridge of boats over the Bay of Naples. He spent much of his time at his huge family estate in the east of Rome, the Horti Lamiani, which included a palace, gardens, pavilions, fountains and myriad sculptures. Since 2022 part of the estate has been visible in a new museum under Piazza Vittorio Emanuele II. Caligula was assassinated in AD 41 and his uncle Claudius succeeded. Sources focus on his reported disabilities or on the unusual way he was proclaimed (pulled by the imperial guards

THE MONUMENTS LEFT BY CLAUDIUS WERE USEFUL RATHER THAN PLENTIFUL

The great Porta Maggiore was a flyover for two major aqueducts over two main roads, making a monument out of the solution to a practical problem. Inscriptions by Claudius and later emperors on the external façade and the interior (shown here) underlined the propaganda importance of such a show of imperial beneficence.

from behind a curtain), but Claudius mended fences with the Senate and shored up the Empire's defences. The monuments he left, according to Suetonius, were useful rather than plentiful. His new deep-water port at Portus, north of Rome's original port of Ostia, was perhaps his greatest achievement, ensuring no future emperor would have to suffer the riots that broke out when the grain barges could not bring in enough corn from Egypt to feed the people. He also worked on Rome's water supply – essential for its growing population – and completed the Aqua Claudia and Aqua Anio Novus aqueducts. All of this contributed to his reputation as a 'good' emperor, and on his death in AD 54 he was deified, the first since Augustus to be so honoured.

Claudius's emphasis on practicality can be seen in the imposing **PORTA MAGGIORE**. With its great façade of deliberately rough-looking 'rusticated' blocks, it is the most striking and unusual gate of Rome. Yet the most interesting feature of the gate was not what passed through it, but what passed over it. The gate was a flyover for two major aqueducts over two main roads, the Via Casilina, south to Monte Cassino and Latium, and the Via Prenestina, southeast towards Praeneste (Palestrina). Both the aqueducts, the Aqua Claudia and the Aqua Anio Novus, were completed by Claudius and this nexus was monumentalized

by him in AD 52, then restored by Vespasian and Titus some twenty to thirty years later. The water channels can be seen where broken open above the gate. Imposing inscriptions ensured the populace knew who to thank for their water supply. Many ancient writers agree that of all the Roman Empire's achievements, its management and provision of water was one of the greatest, and this is best seen in Rome. This mighty project began with the Aqua Appia aqueduct in 312 BC, and by the AD 200s eleven aqueducts brought water to the city for drinking, bathing, entertainment and decoration. They supplied well over a million cubic metres (more than 300,000,000 gallons) every day, making Rome one of the best-watered cities in history. The aqueducts were also remarkable in their structure, exploiting fully the versatility of concrete and the elegant strength of the arch.

In the AD 270s the structure became a gate in Aurelian's city walls, the greenish-brown tufa piers of the aqueducts contrasting with Aurelian's brickwork. The brick infill was in places removed in the 19th century to facilitate the ever-increasing flow of traffic.

Nero (r. AD 54–68) was adopted by Claudius and was the last of Augustus's family to hold imperial power. He began his reign as a popular, adored young prince. He was very well versed

Above: A reconstruction of the countryside to the southeast of Rome, showing the straight structure of Claudius's new aqueducts – the Anio Novus and Claudia – crossed by the curved Aqua Marcia. Rome's aqueducts brought water from as far as 80 km (50 miles) away.

Opposite: At the top of the Porta Maggiore where the structure has fallen away it is possible to see the water channels of the Aqua Anio Novus and Aqua Claudia. Between them they may have met around a fifth of Rome's colossal water needs.

in the arts, composing and performing poetry and music (an imperial first...). In 2023 a small, but sumptuously decorated, theatre was discovered between St Peter's and Castel Sant'Angelo, an area that was part of Nero's palace gardens in antiquity. Was this perhaps Nero's rehearsal venue, mentioned by Pliny? Nero toured the culturally rich Greek east of the Empire, where he took part in contests of music and chariot racing (in the ancient world usually linked to religious festivals) – and, of course, always won. He visited sanctuaries and temples, admired famous works of art, and brought them back to Rome to grace his own residences. But there was a much darker side to Nero – such as his uncomfortably close links to the deaths of two of his wives, and that of his mother Agrippina the Younger. After the Great Fire of AD 64, Nero set up (or allowed to be set up) the Christians as scapegoats and had thousands murdered in terrible ways, including using them as human torches to illuminate games and races. Nero's major architectural legacy arose, in fact, from the Great Fire. Before the fire, he lived in the vast Domus Transitoria, stretching from the Palatine to the site of the future Colosseum. Fragments of its opulent decoration, including extremely fine *opus sectile* (inlaid marble) wall decor, can be viewed in the Palatine Museum. After the catastrophe in AD 64, he appropriated a huge chunk of central Rome to build a new palace, the **DOMUS AUREA** (Golden House), and the **COLOSSUS OF NERO**.

The palace was set in an immense estate comprising parks, gardens and pavilions, covering about 80 hectares (197 acres), approximately one-eighth of the city. One of the principal features was a vast lake, on the future site of the Colosseum, and according to Suetonius, it was a display of utter wastefulness: 'the whole palace was covered with gold and gems.... The formal dining rooms had ivory panelled ceilings with openings from which came flowers and perfume.' One of the dining areas was round and revolved night and day. When the palace was finished Nero is supposed to have said, 'At last I can live like a human being.'

Today, under the remains of the Baths of Trajan, some 150 rooms of the Domus Aurea have been rediscovered. The walls were covered with marble veneer and the ceilings with mosaics and painted stucco. Painted decoration everywhere in the palace, even in humbler service areas, was in the so-called 'fourth Pompeian style' of wall painting popular in the AD 60s and 70s, featuring large blocks of colour alongside small, painstakingly detailed motifs and architectural details.

After Nero's death in AD 68, Vespasian and Titus used the palace (though they filled in the lake and built the Colosseum on its site). Their successor Domitian constructed his own massive palace on the Palatine and in 104 the Domus Aurea was gutted by fire and never rebuilt. Trajan then partly demolished and buried the palace as foundations for his public baths. The palace was rediscovered in the late 15th century, and people from Michelangelo to the Marquis de Sade explored its dark passages and marvelled at its extraordinary decoration. Corridors were buried to such a depth that visitors wrote their names in torch-soot on the vaults. They called the dark, dank spaces 'caves' (Italian *grotte*) and their decoration became known as *grottesche* (cave-like) – the origin of the art historical term 'grotesque'. These busy, florid designs revolutionized the decorative arts, inspiring ceiling and wall decoration in the Vatican and many other palaces.

Renaissance drawings show much of the decoration in good condition, but souvenir-hunting and damp led to severe damage. Humidity and partial collapses caused by the weight of Trajan's Baths above have plagued the Domus Aurea, but part is now visitable. A main feature now is the later, heavy grey foundation walls of Trajan's Baths. In Nero's day these spaces were bright

Previous pages: A reconstruction of Nero's Domus Aurea and its estate. At the top left, the sumptuously decorated palace looks out over vast parklands, formal gardens and pavilions. The great pool, with its pleasure barge, occupies the future site of the Colosseum, while in the immense atrium stands the bronze Colossus of Nero.

FROM BRICK TO MARBLE

Opposite: The octagonal hall was one of the most ornate rooms of the Domus Aurea. Its dome rose ingeniously from an octagonal base – a first in Roman architecture. Probably a dining room, its floors and walls were lined with the finest marble, the dome covered with painted and gilded stucco and beautiful glass mosaics.

Right: A detail of the intricate 'grotesque' style painted decoration that covered the ceilings of the Domus Aurea. Also known as the 'fourth Pompeian' style, it featured scenes surrounded by detailed swirling, fantastical floral motifs, people, animals and architecture. Championed by Raphael it inspired the decoration of many Renaissance buildings.

and airy rooms, with sweeping views to the lake and valley below. There was a great colonnaded courtyard surrounded by at least fifty dining rooms, fountain houses and many other rooms all beautifully decorated.

The most remarkable room so far discovered is the great octagonal hall. In this milestone in Roman architecture, the ceiling changes from an octagonal vault to a true circular dome, complete with a central opening (oculus) – a feature later seen in the Pantheon. Sadly this is not the great revolving dining room – there is simply no space for the necessary mechanism. Excavations in 2009, however, uncovered a large, round structure with features that suggest the accounts were perhaps true after all.

The Domus Aurea had another major feature, which long after the end of the palace remained a wonder of Rome, the Colossus of Nero. This was a towering bronze statue, about 33 m (108 ft) high, of Sol the god of the sun. Nero originally set it up in the vestibule of his palace, naturally replacing Sol's features with his own (though the emperor Titus restored the original face). In the AD 130s Hadrian needed the site for his Temple of Venus and Roma, so he moved the statue to its final site, next to the Flavian Amphitheatre, to which (after the Empire) it gave the name 'Colosseum'. It seems to have survived into the early Middle Ages but was then toppled and melted down, its huge quantities of bronze a tempting target for a zealous pope. Its brick and concrete base, measuring 17.5 × 14.5 m (57 ft 5 in. × 47 ft 6 in.) and still about a metre high, was rediscovered in the 1820s but partly destroyed in the 1930s.

III.

NEW
BUILDERS

THE FIRST FLAVIANS

F OLLOWING THE ASSASSINATION of Nero in AD 68 and
the violent chaos that ensued in 69 – the 'year of the four
emperors' – power finally fell to the last of the four, Vespasian
(r. AD 69–79), and his sons Titus and Domitian, known by their
family name, the Flavians. Vespasian and his older son Titus
(r. AD 79–81) were very successful generals, who worked in
tandem to reunite the Empire, defeating rival armies and putting
down revolts, in particular in Judaea. Having taken Jerusalem
and destroyed the Holy Temple of the Jews, they brought huge
amounts of gold and silver booty back to Rome. This money
funded a major building programme, primarily the Colosseum
and the Forum of Vespasian.

Vespasian respected the Senate and went about repairing
the physical and societal damage of AD 69. On his death, the
well-liked old emperor left his throne to Titus, who at the time
was wildly unpopular – considered by many to be his father's
henchman and responsible for a wave of banishments, treason
trials and confiscations (and guilty of a shocking affair with
the queen of Judaea). However, his speedy and humane reaction
to two disasters in AD 79, the destruction of Pompeii in the
catastrophic eruption of Mount Vesuvius and a massive fire
in Rome, rehabilitated his reputation. His building record was
intertwined with his father's – finishing off monuments such
as the Colosseum and the Forum of Peace. Nevertheless, by the
time of his death Suetonius could describe Titus as 'the darling
and delight of the whole human race'.

The **FORUM OF VESPASIAN** was very different from those
of Caesar or Augustus. Their forums were principally for the
administration of law, but Vespasian's was to be a place of culture,

VESPASIAN'S
FORUM WAS
A PLACE
OF CULTURE,
A MUSEUM,
SET IN A ROSE
GARDEN

Reconstruction of the Forum of Vespasian. Unlike other imperial forums this was a place not of commerce but of culture, with its water, greenery, and Temple of Peace (centre). The piazza was filled with long marble channels, lined with rose bushes, from which water flowed out creating modern-style water curtains.

and contemplation, a form of museum, bringing together famous works from all over the known world, in particular Greece. And he placed his museum in a great, well-watered rose garden.

The Forum was dedicated in AD 75 by Vespasian, on the site of the great Republican market or *macellum*. It comprised, in common with other imperial forums, a vast colonnaded square, approximately 110 × 110 m (361 × 361 ft), with columns of pink Egyptian granite, but excavations have revealed several unique features. Most of the piazza was not paved, but had a beaten earth surface, with paving only in some parts, and two sets of three long brick features. Deep marble drainage channels around them suggest they were ornamental water cascades, similar to those seen today in public places, rather than the foundations for flower beds or market stalls. A garden element was provided by rose bushes that lined the water features, planted out in the bottoms of reused wine amphorae.

Like the Forums of Caesar and Augustus, Vespasian's too had a formal temple as its main focus, the Temple of Peace, but it was

located within the eastern (Colosseum) colonnade. Six gigantic granite columns almost 15 m (49 ft) high led to an apsidal *exedra*, containing the cult statue of Peace. It was flanked by rooms containing a library, archives and a dazzling array of art. Among its treasures was the booty from the Jewish Temple at Jerusalem, including the Great Menorah (the sacred seven-branched candelabrum). This features on a relief on the Arch of Titus, showing the triumph after the fall of Jerusalem. The menorah's journey shows how in the ancient world (as now) art and culture were at the mercy of the fortunes of war. In AD 455, Vandals took the menorah to their capital of Carthage, from where the Byzantine general Belisarius, in 534, took it to Constantinople and gave it to the emperor Justinian. He sent it back to Jerusalem (though to Christian priests), where it finally disappeared in the sack of the city by the Persians in 614. Some conspiracy theories suggest that it never left Rome and now resides in the Vatican.

The whole complex was filled with bronze and marble statues, including a great bronze bull of the 5th century BC by Pheidias, the Greek master sculptor of Athena Parthenos. Most had been looted from Greece by Nero to decorate his Domus Aurea, but Vespasian's Forum brought them back into the public domain. The Temple itself had already disappeared by about AD 500, whether through lightning, earthquake, age or deliberate demolition, but the host of statues remained. A historian in the 6th century pictures the temple-less Forum, with cattle being driven across the piazza, one of them dallying with Pheidias's realistic bull.

A large square hall in the southwest of the Forum, now the façade of the church of Santi Cosma e Damiano, once housed urban surveyors' archives after the fires of AD 64 and 69. All the plans and registers to deeds of title to all premises and land were stored here. Built of solid stone with a concrete vaulted roof to make it supposedly fireproof, the building, known as Templum Sacrae Urbis (the Temple of the Sacred City), was rebuilt at least twice after serious fires.

Septimius Severus rebuilt the hall in the early 3rd century, richly redecorating it with wall panels of finely cut marble, showing the legendary history of Rome. In the AD 530s it was converted into the church of Santi Cosma e Damiano, but remained remarkably intact, down to its marble niches and shelves for the archives and records. Sadly in the 1630s Pope Urban VIII raised the floor level, selling or destroying all the decoration and fittings. On an interior wall was

THE FORMA URBIS WAS A HUGE MARBLE PLAN OF THE WHOLE CITY, SHOWING EVERYTHING FROM TEMPLES TO TENEMENT BLOCKS

The Forum also housed the Templum Sacrae Urbis (Temple of the Sacred City), which stored Rome's archive of property plans and records. On one wall of the Temple was the great *forma urbis* – a huge marble plan of the whole city. It showed administrative districts, streets, public buildings, tenement blocks and even private houses in remarkable detail.

Septimius Severus's huge plan of the city, the *forma urbis* (plan of Rome), on sheets of marble totalling 235 sq. m (2,530 sq. ft), at a scale of approximately 1:250. Approximately one-tenth has survived, though small pieces were discovered as recently as AD 2000, and more may emerge. The wall is still studded with holes for the clamps that held the marble sheets in place.

Excavations in front of the church in 2006 revealed the Temple's original flooring in squares and circles of coloured marble, and part of the forum piazza, steps and granite colonnades. The floor is pitted with cisterns or vats, suggesting the Forum, in its later history, might have been used for shops, markets and industrial workshops as the ancient world morphed gradually into the Middle Ages.

Beyond the Arch of Titus, at the end of the Forum, looms the building that has for almost two millennia been the most enduring symbol of Rome, the COLOSSEUM. For many people the Colosseum is the most memorable sight of the city, an icon for Rome itself. It was the Roman world's largest amphitheatre – a large, purpose-built oval structure for gladiatorial combat and beast fights. It did not gain the name Colosseum until the early Middle Ages. The Romans called it the 'Amphitheatrum Flavium' after the Flavian dynasty that built it. Nor was it the first amphitheatre in Rome. That was erected in 52 BC and was literally an *amphi theatre* (double theatres), made of two wooden semi-circular theatres pivoted together to become one great oval. A stone amphitheatre was built in Rome in 29 BC, but was destroyed in the Fire of Nero.

The Colosseum stands on the site originally occupied by the ornamental pool of Nero's Domus Aurea. Construction began under Vespasian in AD 70, and was finished by his son Titus in AD 80. At first it had only three storeys. The fourth was added by Domitian, who also replaced the earthen surface with a wooden floor, today partly reconstructed (and perhaps to be fully rebuilt in the future). The sand (in Latin *harena*) spread over this floor, to soak up the blood, lent the name 'arena'. Below was a labyrinth of passageways, the hypogeum, with cages and cells for people and animals, and lifts and other ingenious devices thanks to which tableaux and landscapes could suddenly appear.

The Colosseum was enormous – 189 m (620 ft) long by 156 m (512 ft) wide, and 48 m (157 ft) high, while the arena itself measured 83 × 48 m (272 × 157 ft). Its construction consumed many thousands of tons of materials, including 100,000 cubic m (3,531,470 cubic ft) of travertine stone for facing and strengthening, massive quantities of brick and concrete for vaults and substructures and 300 tons of iron just for masonry clamps. It was the clamps' removal that pitted the exterior, and weakened the structure so fatally. The ruins today show 'all the workings'. Where the travertine surface has fallen away, it reveals the source of the Colosseum's success – the triumph of brick and concrete, giving that important combination of lightness and strength.

The exterior façade is decorated with Tuscan, Ionic and Corinthian columns and pilasters, and on the top level were supports for wooden masts for the *velarium*, an immense awning

THE COLOSSEUM HAS FOR ALMOST TWO MILLENNIA BEEN THE MOST ENDURING SYMBOL OF ROME

Opposite: The Colosseum, seen here from its best-preserved, northern side, was the largest arena in the Roman world. Known to the Romans as the Amphitheatrum Flavium, it was a perfect propaganda monument. Inscriptions proclaimed it was built with the gold from the conquered province of Judaea – emphasizing the power of Rome and its emperors.

Overleaf: Reconstruction of the Colosseum in the AD 330s. Spectators came in through numbered entrances to take their allotted, socially stratified, seats. Visible at the top is the network of ropes used to operate the great canvas awning (*velarium*). Bottom right is the Colossus of Nero; to the left, and all around, were stalls selling food, drink and souvenirs.

to protect spectators from the sun. Sailors, used to handling rigging and stationed in special barracks nearby, were enlisted to operate the *velarium*.

No full account survives of a day in the arena, but various writers suggest possible schedules. For days before the games, advertisements were painted on walls and handbills distributed, detailing fighters, schedules and whether the awnings would be raised or not. The games were politically and socially very important, and sponsors gained favour with the crowd (and more so as the number and quality of beasts and gladiators grew). Given the prestige and cost of the games, it is unsurprising that in Rome they became the monopoly of the emperors.

Events began with a procession, or *pompa*, a gladiator (and beast and hunter) parade – all to stirring music from drums, trumpets, flutes and water organs. Lighter entertainments came first, with gymnasts, jugglers, acrobats – both human and animal. Things took a bloodier turn with combats between animals, or animals and specially trained hunters – not gladiators, who never fought animals, but *venatores*. Then came executions

of *noxii*, criminals guilty of major crimes such as treason or defiling a temple. These prisoners, enemies of Rome and civil order, could be condemned *ad bestias* (to be torn apart by wild animals) or *ad flammas* (to be burned alive).

Animals were key to the entertainments in the arena, and ever larger numbers of increasingly exotic animals from all over the Empire and beyond were needed, at enormous expense. For the dedication of the Colosseum, Titus gave over 100 days of lavish entertainments and thousands of animals were killed, including elephants, bears, lions and a rhinoceros. Even in the troubled 3rd century AD, the emperor Probus in AD 281 displayed – and despatched – hundreds of lions, bears and leopards.

In the afternoon came the climax of the day's events, the gladiators. They perhaps first performed at funerals in central and southern Italy, to glorify the deceased and pacify blood-thirsty spirits. Imported to Rome in the 260s BC they quickly became popular at wealthy funerals and other occasions, originally fighting in open areas – even the Forum – but from the 1st century BC increasingly in a purpose-built arena. Gladiator bouts became an indispensable part of the calendar, and entertainments became lengthier as animal combats were introduced.

The vast majority of gladiators, as so much of the population of Rome and the Empire, were enslaved persons, with no rights. Their owners kept and trained them in a special barracks, the *ludus*. The most famous *ludi* were in Rome and Capua, where the rebel gladiator Spartacus learnt his skills. Gladiators trained in particular fighting styles, such as the *thraex* (Thracian) or the *retiarius* (net-fighter), with specific weapons and combat methods. Certain pairs of gladiators were matched, such as the *retiarius* with the *secutor* (chaser), which made fights more balanced and interesting. As well as blood, the crowd wanted to see skill and expertise, so gladiators did not always fight to the death (they were, after all, a valuable, highly trained resource).

An interesting dynamic arose at the end of a fight. Assuming the losing gladiator had not been killed outright, then the emperor, the most powerful man in the world, had to decide his fate. He turned to the crowd and for that moment they had the power (it was a very unwise emperor who would go against the voice of 60,000 people...). So gladiators could leave the arena honourably, even if defeated, provided they fought bravely and pleased the crowd. If they won a fight their owner usually allowed them to keep some of the prize money. Many gladiators retired, famous and wealthy men, to own and train their own gladiators.

A relief from Smyrna (Izmir), Turkey, shows chained prisoners led by armed men. These are probably *noxii* – prisoners of war or those convicted of major crimes, enslaved and condemned to die in the arena. Unlike gladiators who could win the crowd's admiration with skill and bravery, the unfortunate *noxii* were usually unarmed and exposed to ferocious, starved animals – a reminder to abide by the Empire's rules.

The helmet of a gladiator known as a *thraex* or Thracian. Although they were slaves, gladiators were admired for their Roman *virtus* (manly bravery). They trained and fought as a particular gladiator with specific armour and weaponry: the Thracian's weapon was a vicious curved sword. This helmet, decorated with the head of Medusa and dolphins, was one of many pieces of armour discovered in the gladiators' barracks in Pompeii in the 1760s.

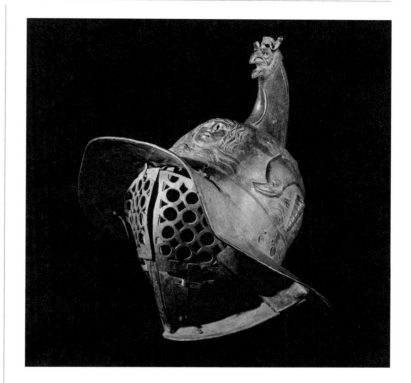

Not only men…though rare, there were some female gladiators, for example Amazon and Achillia shown on a relief in the British Museum from Halicarnassus (Bodrum in modern Turkey).

Gladiators (along with charioteers), though slaves, were media stars and, yes, sex symbols. Their manly fighting skills and physical attractiveness made them favourites with the people. Juvenal writes of Eppia, a senator's wife, who ran away to Egypt with her gladiator lover Sergius. He had an infected wound, various scars and sores and a nasty runny eye – but he was a gladiator!

The impact of the Colosseum was immense. During its construction, thousands of people and animals laboured for a decade amid a mountain of building materials. The completed Colosseum regularly drew in people and animals for the arena and tens of thousands of spectators, and the local area had to provide the necessary infrastructure to feed and water them. In the early 2020s, archaeologists excavating the drains under the Colosseum found the bones of animals including lions and bears, presumably slaughtered in the arena, and the remains of nuts, cherries, peaches and other snacks that the audience had enjoyed during the 'entertainments'. To the physical presence of the monument and the crowds add the strong, unpleasant smells from hundreds of animals penned below, or dying eviscerated on the sand, then the noise – the volume and intensity (and vibration?) would have been extraordinary. And all right in the heart of the city, next to the Forum Romanum itself.

The Colosseum had a long, chequered history. On the interior of the upper storey reused masonry (*spolia*) shows repairs after a lightning strike in AD 217 (events were temporarily transferred to the Circus Maximus). Inscriptions record repairs several times in the 5th and early 6th centuries AD, but the games became increasingly unsustainable as costs rocketed and animals and gladiators became scarcer. In any case, society was changing and gladiators were banned by Christian emperors in the early 5th century, with the last animal combats in 523. Excavations show the Colosseum quickly fell into total disrepair, filling with refuse and rubble. But it still captured the imagination. The British monk Bede, writing in the AD 720s, said, 'As long as the Colosseum stands Rome shall stand; when the Colosseum falls, Rome too shall fall, and when Rome falls, with it shall fall the world.'

In the Middle Ages the Colosseum became a fortress, invaded by houses, shops, churches and even a graveyard. It remained fairly intact until a major earthquake (probably in 1349) brought down much of the south side, weakened by the removal of iron masonry clamps. Excavations in 2022–23 uncovered the massive footprint of that collapsed section. The resulting mini-mountain of stone was quarried for centuries,

SEATING HIERARCHY

THE PUBLIC, AT full capacity around 60,000 of them, came into the Colosseum through eighty arched entrances, with Latin identification numerals still visible, and sat in allotted areas. Entrance was free as the events were sponsored – their Latin name was *munera*, literally 'gifts' – but quality and placing of seating depended on social status. The emperor, priests, Vestal Virgins and senators took the seats nearest the arena, then *equites* (the knights) and other VIPs, followed by ordinary citizens and finally, on the highest tier, on wooden benches under a portico, slaves, non-citizens and women. There are also examples of reserved, 'corporate' places – inscribed marble seating blocks for certain trade guilds and foreign dignitaries. The arena was in effect a microcosm of Roman society, with its layers of privilege and power, and the spectators, too, were a cosmopolitan slice of the Empire and its peoples.

The interior of the Colosseum today. Centuries of decay and stone robbing have left only its skeleton, but they have exposed its workings. Beneath the arena was a complex undercroft, or *hypogeum*, containing lifts and trap doors that could suddenly throw up into the arena people and animals, even stage sets of whole provinces.

providing stone for churches and palaces, including St Peter's, and the Capitoline Museums. In 1452 one contractor alone carried away 2,500 cartloads of stone. The interior was also ruthlessly plundered, leaving only the concrete skeleton seen today. Quarrying of the Colosseum ceased in the late 17th century, when the popes consecrated it to the 'Christian Martyrs', and a century or so later built buttresses at the 'frayed' ends of its arcades – which otherwise would have fallen in a domino effect.

The Colosseum's romantic ruins inspired artists from writers, such as Goethe and Byron, to painters including Canaletto and Turner. A part of the attraction was the incredible array of flora that flourished in the ruins. Some 420 different species were catalogued in 1855 by the English botanist Henry Deakin in *Flora of the Colosseum*, but sadly, all were stripped away in the 1870s.

Today the Colosseum in ruin is still much more impressive than many other buildings in their prime, and its impact on

Opposite: The Arch of Titus, stands at the eastern entrance to the Forum Romanum. Built in the AD 80s by Domitian, its grand inscription, once filled with bronze letters, dedicates it to his brother, the deified Titus, and their father the deified Vespasian.

Below: The decoration on the interior of the Arch of Titus preserves reliefs of scenes from the triumph celebrated by Titus and Vespasian after their conquest of Judaea. This panel shows soldiers carrying two of the great treasures of the Temple at Jerusalem: the table of showbread and, on the left, the Great Menorah.

visitors is perhaps just as powerful as it was in ancient times. Into this monument, of all Rome's monuments, people come with their expectations, prejudices and cultural identifications. Some are exhilarated by the sense of history and the almost tangible presence of the ancient Romans – with the emperor and all Roman society ranged around and the crowd roaring at events unfolding below. For others there is a sense of real foreboding, a horror at the cruel slaughter of humans and animals that took place, and incomprehension at the ability of the Romans to enjoy it all so much and place it so centrally in their society.

Whatever its history means to each visitor, the Colosseum remains one of the most impressive and powerful monuments of Rome and is key to understanding so much of the ancient city.

At the crest of the Via Sacra at the east end of the Forum, a symbol in many ways of the Forum area, is the **ARCH OF TITUS**. Standing 13.5 m (more than 44 ft) wide and 15.5 m (nearly 51 ft) high, it was dedicated by the emperor Domitian in the AD 80s in memory of his brother Titus (r. AD 79–81), who is described as DIVUS, or deified, proving the monument was posthumous. The inscription facing the Colosseum carries in full the dedication 'SENATUS POPULUSQUE ROMANUS' (The Senate and the Roman People, normally abbreviated to SPQR) and

commemorates Titus and his father Vespasian. The Arch celebrates their victory over the Jews in AD 70, and the spectacular triumphal procession held afterwards in Rome. The whole triumph was originally depicted in a narrow relief which continued around all sides but is preserved only above the Arch on the east (facing the Colosseum). Larger panels in very high relief, and still fairly well preserved, decorate the interior. These show on one side the display of booty from the Great Temple at Jerusalem including the Great Menorah. Other soldiers carry *tabulae* (placards) which in the real triumph bore painted names and images of captured cities and peoples. A group of soldiers carries a squared object on a litter supported by poles on their shoulders, perhaps the Table of Showbread. The menorah and other treasures were taken to Vespasian's Forum and deposited in his Temple of Peace, remaining there for over 400 years. On the other side appears a chariot containing Titus, crowned by Victory, while the goddess Roma herself leads the horses. On the vault inside the Arch, Titus rides to heaven on an eagle at the moment of his *apotheosis* (deification) surrounded by coffering and flowers. In Roman times the Forum was filled not only with the monuments whose remains we see today but many other buildings, shrines and statues, which have completely vanished. One of the most spectacular of these, near the Arch of Titus, was a group of life-sized bronze elephants, which still survived into the 6th century AD.

By the early 19th-century the Arch of Titus, built of fine Pentelic marble from Athens, was in extremely bad condition – aggravated by the demolition of adjoining structures that had propped it up. In the 1820s it was completely restored, with damaged or missing marble replaced with local travertine. This view of the Arch in the late 19th century shows clearly the more weathered original, central area and the two cleaner sides, replaced in the restoration.

An early 19th century view of the Arch of Titus shows how much of what had been the ancient city of Rome became rural – a reality that continued well into that century. Above the people in traditional costume is a panel showing Titus in glory. The emperor in his chariot, accompanied by the goddess Victory, leads his triumphal procession to celebrate the suppression of the Jewish Revolt. Oblivious to these past glories, the people go about their daily lives.

In the Middle Ages the Arch of Titus was converted into a fortress by the Frangipani family. Houses and other structures were subsequently built against (and on) it, but were partly removed in the later Middle Ages. In the 1820s the whole structure, in a very perilous state, was completely dismantled and rebuilt by the archaeologist Giuseppe Valadier, on behalf of Pope Pius VII. The reconstruction was particularly thorough on the west side (facing the Forum). Local travertine limestone, with its distinctive pitted surface, was used to fill the gaps in the original Greek Pentelic marble.

DOMITIAN

(R. AD 81–96)

AFTER THE DEATHS of his father Vespasian and brother Titus, Domitian came to the throne in AD 81. His reign started well, with important victories on the Rhine and Danube frontiers and a new drive for public and private morality, reform of the civil service and many areas of Roman life. Sadly this went out of control, with several Vestals condemned to death and a purge, amounting to a reign of terror, unleashed against real and perceived critics and enemies. With the Senate and many others against him (even his empress Domitia), he was assassinated in AD 96.

Domitian continued the Flavian building boom, becoming one of the great imperial builders. Along with the Arch dedicated to his deified brother Titus, he built the Temple to Titus and Vespasian nestling under the great Tabularium (record office) in the Forum Romanum. In his own right he built the fourth imperial forum (though it never bore his name), and restored the Temple of Jupiter Optimus Maximus and the House of the Vestals. He also built the immense imperial palace on the Palatine and something revolutionary, a great stadium – a venue for Greek-style athletic contests – in the Campus Martius. Unfortunately his architectural legacy was largely overshadowed by his squalid assassination by some of his own imperial staff (one of whom was a former gladiator) and condemnation by the Senate, which hated him and certainly played a part in his death. His popularity with the army could not, in this case, save him. The Senate's condemnation was the exact opposite of deification or apotheosis, in which the person was transported to the gods in heaven and their memory was glorified on Earth. Domitian simply ceased to be. Suetonius relates how the people

> THE PEOPLE 'CALLED FOR LADDERS TO PULL DOWN OBJECTS LINKED TO THE EMPEROR AND WATCHED THEM FALL TO EARTH'
>
> SUETONIUS

A statue of a Vestal priestess wearing the characteristic *seni crines* (six-tressed) hairstyle. Her head is covered by the *suffibulum*, a shoulder-length veil, which would have been white with a purple border, clasped with a brooch. Her long, flowing robe (*stola*) is bound below the breast with a woollen belt tied with a Hercules knot.

'...called for ladders to pull down objects linked to the emperor and watched them fall to earth and smash. By senatorial decree all his inscriptions were to be similarly erased or destroyed and any memory of him obliterated'.

Next to the Temple of Vesta in the heart of the Forum Romanum, Domitian rebuilt the **HOUSE OF THE VESTALS**, the Atrium Vestae. This huge residence housed the serving Vestals, initiates, retired Vestals who remained in the priesthood, and numerous slaves. A two-storey colonnade surrounded a great courtyard of 61 × 20 m (200 × 65½ ft), with dining rooms, a bath suite and a bakery (for making the special sacred cakes for official sacrifices). Parts of the ground floor still remain, around two central pools surrounded by statues and bases dedicated to senior Vestals. Originally there were around a hundred of these sculptures, but only thirty survive – and these only by a quirk of fate. They were discovered in the 19th century by the Italian archaeologist Rodolfo Lanciani, in an undignified heap in a lime-kiln on the south side of the courtyard. We have no idea why this particular kiln full of statuary had not been fired up, but nearby spreads of ash and lime showed how the other statues had perished.

Only one statue of a Vestal in the courtyard was found with its base – Flavia Publicia, a senior Vestal of the mid-3rd century AD. She was described by Lanciani as 'of tall, queenly appearance of noble demeanour, of a sweet and gentle, if not handsome, face'. The last senior Vestal was Coelia Concordia, appointed in the 380s, and a vehement opponent of Christianity. A legend recounts how in the 390s an imperial princess came to the Temple of Vesta (now closed, as all temples, by imperial decree) and took a necklace from a statue of the goddess. Concordia cursed the princess, who met an unpleasant and untimely death.

After the closure of the pagan cults, the House of the Vestals was abandoned, and then was gradually transformed in the 6th and 7th centuries into numerous private homes. A hoard of English coins buried here in the 10th century AD shows Rome's continued importance in trade (and religion) even after the Empire fell. Like much of the Forum area, the House of the Vestals was thoroughly ransacked for materials for the new St Peter's Basilica in 1540.

One of Domitian's most striking monuments is the **STADIUM OF DOMITIAN**, located at Piazza Navona. This distinctive, elongated piazza, with its southern end flattened and the northern curved, has this peculiar shape today because

it was built directly over the remains of the *stadium* or athletics venue of Domitian, built in the AD 80s. As well as the shape, the name also recalls the Stadium, as Navona is almost certainly derived from *in agonis*, 'at the contests'.

The Stadium of Domitian was approximately 275 m (902 ft) long by 106 m (348 ft) wide, and could seat around 30,000 people. Its exterior presented a two-tier arcade in gleaming travertine, decorated with Ionic and Corinthian architecture, as on the Colosseum. This structure was built for very different entertainments, however – athletics competitions such as running, wrestling, boxing and discus. Games were held in honour of Jupiter Capitolinus and all were conducted in Greek style (with competitors naked). Septimius Severus introduced female participants – but then banned them because of the crowd's ribald comments. The Stadium hosted gladiators when the Colosseum was out of action and also saw executions of criminals and other enemies of the state, such as Christians. In AD 303 St Agnes was supposedly martyred in one of the brothels that sprang up around the arcades of the Stadium, as they did around other entertainment venues such as the Circus Maximus (so much so that in the AD 220s Severus Alexander placed a tax on the pimps and prostitutes haunting the arches, in order to fund repairs to arcaded public buildings).

Much of the structure and seating survived intact until the building was extensively quarried in the early 16th century.

Previous pages: Aerial view of Piazza Navona, which preserves perfectly the shape of the Stadium of Domitian that lies beneath it. He built it as a venue for gymnastics such as boxing and running. Now the piazza hosts numerous buildings including the church of Saint Agnes, who was martyred near the Stadium in the early 300s.

Below: An 18th-century painting of the 'lake' of Piazza Navona. From 1652, the popes decided to flood the square on August weekends, both as a novelty and to help relieve Rome's excessive heat. The outflow of the square's fountains were blocked and water filled the (then concave) centre. The rich then rode their carriages (or rowed their boats) around the lake while the poor washed and splashed. The custom lasted until 1865.

NEW BUILDERS

Overleaf: Reconstruction of the Forum of Nerva in AD 100. Although dedicated by and named for Nerva, the Forum and its Temple of Minerva were built by Domitian. It was squeezed in between other forums, narrow and very long, stretching as far as the Curia and this thoroughfare feel was increased by the Argiletum road that ran through it. It was nonetheless richly decorated, notably with a brightly painted frieze, hundreds of metres long, celebrating Minerva.

But houses and churches retained the stadium shape and the piazza remained a centre for meeting and recreation. From 1652 until 1865 its centre was flooded on August weekends with water from the Roman aqueduct, the Aqua Virgo (Italian Acqua Vergine). People rode around this 'lake' in their carriages, past the fountain of the rivers, with its obelisk (coincidentally brought to Rome by Domitian) towering over them.

Part of the north (rounded) end of the Stadium was revealed in the 1930s and can now be visited. Excavations exposed an entrance with great structural pilasters of travertine, as well as brick and concrete walls that formed the dividing 'wedges', as well as vaulting for the upper floors and stairways up to the second level. Some brick pilasters have traces of thick plaster coating, grooved to resemble marble veneer. The niches were once filled with statues, and one contains a sad illustration of their fate – two marble feet from two different statues, the rest long since reduced to builders' lime.

Because of the Senate's condemnation of him, Domitian's Forum was never known as such. Instead it became the **FORUM OF NERVA,** the respected diplomat and statesman who reigned after him. It was also called the 'Forum Transitorium' because it incorporated the Argiletum, an ancient road which passed from the inner city quarter, the Subura, through the Forum Romanum and down towards the River Tiber. Underneath it here, and following more or less its full route, was the great drain or Cloaca Maxima.

The Forum site was effectively squeezed on both long sides, by the Forum of Augustus to the left and the Forum of Vespasian and Temple of Peace to the right. To the rear was the Subura and to the front were the Basilica Aemilia and the Forum Romanum. Its proportions (117 × 39 m; 384 × 128 ft) were long but so narrow that the colonnades had to be placed close against the side walls and could not serve as true shaded walkways. In the early 3rd century, the emperor Alexander Severus restricted space still further, by filling the Forum with statues of all the deified emperors and empresses. The focus of the Forum was the Temple of Minerva, the patron deity of Domitian. The frieze that ran along the top of the colonnade showed scenes from the life of the Minerva, emphasizing her role as goddess of crafts and, by association, protector of women and the home.

The Temple of Minerva and much of the Forum colonnades remained substantially intact into the Middle Ages and were described by an English monk, Magister Gregory, in the 12th century. He said the Temple of Minerva '...was once an

IMP·NERVA·CAESAR·AVG·GERMANICVS·PONT·MAX
TRIB·POTE ST·II·COS·III·P·P·AEDEM·MINERVAE·FECIT

outstanding building, but it was pulled down with great effort by the Christians and also fell into ruin because of great age… what remains is now the grain storehouse of the Cardinals. Here is a great heap of broken effigies, and here a headless image of Pallas, armed, standing on the pediment, a marvel to behold.'

Prints of the late 16th century show the Temple was still more than half-complete, but in 1606 it was utterly destroyed for stone to decorate a fountain on the Janiculum Hill.

The remains of the temple podium, comprising a great low concrete and brick arch, and blocks of travertine and greenish tufa lower down, are overlooked on the right by the only two remaining columns of the colonnades, called for centuries *Le colonnacce* – 'the scraggy old columns'. Above these, the remaining part of the frieze, carved in high relief and of very fine quality, shows on the upper level a female figure, perhaps Minerva, and below, women and domestic activities. It was also brightly painted, like most Classical Greek and Roman sculptures.

A visitor looking down into the Forum, at the foot of the *colonnacce*, can make out traces of the road, heavily scored with wheel ruts carved over the centuries into the tufa surface.

A reconstruction of the Forum of Nerva in around AD 900. Archaeologists excavating in the 1990s found remains of two-storey medieval houses facing onto a road that still respected the original Forum paving. Although the area within the Forum walls was now given over to agriculture, evidence suggests the perimeter walls, colonnades and the Temple were all still largely intact. In fact, the Temple stood until 1606 when it was demolished for stone to make a fountain.

THE TEMPLE OF MINERVA 'WAS ONCE AN OUTSTANDING BUILDING... WHAT REMAINS IS NOW THE GRAIN STOREHOUSE OF THE CARDINALS'

MAGISTER GREGORY

Le Colonnacce – the 'raggedy old columns' – is all that remains of the colonnade that surrounded the Forum piazza. The large female figure (possibly Minerva) is clearly visible, a lucky survival from the beautifully carved frieze. After the Forum's twilight years as a farming village, the lime-kilns moved in and columns, frieze and veneer blocks were all burnt for lime.

Excavations in the mid-1990s revealed a fascinating glimpse of life after the Empire. On the remains of the Forum paving, next to the rutted Argiletum road, were found the substantial remains of a large, arcaded house dating to the 9th century. And there were others, all at the level of the Forum paving, suggesting this forum, unlike many other parts of the Roman monumental city, was still in some way used. In the 9th century AD a community lived and farmed here, within its intact, beautifully decorated Roman walls.

The **PALACE OF DOMITIAN**, constructed throughout the AD 80s and 90s, was one of the most extensive and lavish building projects the city had seen. Contemporary writers said its architect Rabirius had brought the heavens to Earth with columns so numerous and mighty they could hold up the gods themselves. Sadly, Domitian, increasingly paranoid (and rightly so, as later proven), had to be careful even in paradise, and some of the palace's corridors and porticoes were lined with mirror-like moonstone, to thwart potential assassins.

The palace covered most of the Palatine Hill, and is today broadly divided into the Domus Flavia, or Flavian House (named after Domitian's family), where the emperor conducted state business, and the Domus Augustana, the House of Majesty (not to be confused with the House of Augustus, also on the Palatine), which was the imperial residence.

At the heart of the Domus Flavia was a vast colonnaded square, with a large central octagonal maze, filled with fountains. To the right was an immense banqueting room for state occasions, with a painted and gilded ceiling around 30.5 m (100 ft) high, tiers of engaged columns and sumptuous veneer. The Roman writer Statius called this 'Iovis Cenatio' – a formal dining hall worthy of Jupiter himself. Its opulence did not save the emperor Pertinax who, amid all this luxury, was cornered and butchered here by disgruntled soldiers in AD 193.

Above: A view, looking east from the Circus Maximus, towards the imperial palaces on the Palatine Hill, including the Palace of Domitian. The buildings visible here are largely substructures and service areas, but the state rooms and living areas were of a beauty and scale unsurpassed.

NEW BUILDERS

Overleaf: A reconstruction of the Aula Regia or Royal Hall of Domitian's Palace. Here on his throne, visible in the central apse, Domitian received visitors as *dominus et deus* (lord and god). Problematic for Romans, since emperors were deified after death, a living god was more difficult to stomach.

Elements of the floor, with its beautiful polychrome squares and circles, remain, teetering and undulating on the piers of a heating system or hypocaust – even Rome is cold in the winter. To left and right, through large, glazed windows, were courtyards with boat-shaped fountains, providing a focal point but also cooling the area in the summer.

A feast for all the senses, dining here was a key function of the imperial diplomatic machine. Banquets were frequent and luxurious, and an army of slaves took care of procuring, cooking and serving food and wine and of the vessels, linen and other

accoutrements. Slavery, repugnant to us, was fundamental to Rome. Evidence for the numbers and range of enslaved people owned by the emperor Augustus and his wife Livia comes from their *columbaria* – burial chambers outside Rome on the Appian Way with multiple niches, resembling nesting places for doves (*columbae*). Inscriptions provide evidence for around 6,000 slaves and freedmen/women, often connected to the dining room. There was a guild of the emperor's cooks, *collegium cocorum Caesaris*; a head chef, *praepositus cocorum*; a superintendent of silver drinking ware, *praepositus argenti potorii*; a keeper of lamps; and many others.

But dining was only one aspect of the work of Palace slaves. In the same *columbaria* were inscriptions to the *purpura* (keeper of imperial purple robes), *ad unguenta* (keeper of perfumes), several *margaritarii* (jewellers), *calciator* (maker of and carer for shoes) and a *supra medicos* (medical supervisor). Plus of course those people – slaves or freed slaves themselves – who organized all of the others.

On the other side of the courtyard were three large rooms. An immense reception hall or throne room was named *aula regia* (the royal hall) by early excavators. Here Domitian received his subjects as *dominus et deus* (lord and god). It was a truly heavenly

The sunken stadium at the eastern side of the Palace of Domitian. The marble-veneered pilasters supported a viewing balcony, and in the east side was a massive, *exedra* (apse), perhaps a 'royal box' from which to contemplate or spectate. What exactly, we do not know. It may have been a sunken garden, though the shape suggests horse racing and a small inset arena may have been for gladiator or beast fights.

NEW BUILDERS

This colossal statue of the god Bacchus, made of rare green basalt from Egypt, stands about 3.5 m (11 ½ ft) tall. It once decorated the Aula Regia of Domitian's palace and, together with a colossal statue of Hercules, was discovered lying on the floor of the hall when it was excavated in the 1720s. The Duke of Parma, a member of the Farnese family, led the excavations and removed the statues to Parma, where they are still displayed.

place, its coffered ceiling floating 30 m (98 ft) above and the walls filled with the finest statues. Two 3.5 m-high (11½ ft) sculptures of Hercules and Bacchus in hard Egyptian green stone found here are now in the Museum of Parma in northern Italy. So impressive was this hall that in AD 629, long after the Western Empire had gone, the Eastern emperor Heraclius was crowned here. On the left is the smaller, apsidal 'basilica', perhaps the *auditorium* or council chamber where the emperor made important decisions away from the meddlesome Senate. On the right is the so-called *lararium*, or shrine of the gods, more likely linked to palace security.

Beyond the state rooms was the private, luxurious, domestic area, the Domus Augustana. At its heart was a sunken courtyard, two storeys deep, with a central monumental fountain. Leading off from the court was a warren of rooms, passages and access corridors which run underneath the entire Palace. Nearby a great curved wall marks the southern façade, from where there were stunning views over the enormous, elongated expanse of the Circus Maximus – now just grassy banks with a dirt track at the centre.

The whole eastern side of the complex was taken up by a sunken two-storeyed stadium, or hippodrome. In this opulent structure, the brickwork of the pilasters was covered not with moulded plaster, but with curved marble plaques. At the centre of the far wall was a great three tiered *exedra* filled with sculptures and frescoes, its uppermost storey a spectacular viewpoint for events in the area below.

The purpose of this sunken area is uncertain, though entertainment seems likely. There was a raised central reserve or *spina*, as in the Circus Maximus, so it may have housed races – for horses rather than chariots, given its size. Others think it was a sunken garden, with plants and trees creating a private imperial park. The small, oval structure at the end looks like an arena, though it was restored at the time of the Germanic kings in the AD 490s, by which time gladiators were officially banned. Perhaps it was for animal combats, which survived well into the 6th century. For the ruler in his palace all was possible.

IV.

ROME IN GLORY

TRAJAN

(R. AD 98–117)

F OLLOWING THE ASSASSINATION and condemnation of Domitian, the throne passed briefly to the respected elder statesman Nerva, who had risen through the imperial diplomatic and civil service. He stabilized the state and even left an architectural legacy (by dedicating Domitian's Forum in his own name). However, he never regained the army's confidence after his perceived involvement in Domitian's murder and rapidly adopted Trajan as his successor. Of Spanish origins, Trajan, the first non-Italian emperor, was a very successful general who expanded the Roman Empire to its greatest extent, conquering Dacia (Romania) and Mesopotamia (Iraq). With the booty from Dacia he launched a huge building programme, including the construction of a massive new harbour and canal complex at Claudius's port of Portus, the complete restructuring of the Circus Maximus, and the building of the immense Trajan's Forum. These constructions transformed the city and the lives of its inhabitants, by providing extra space for new or existing activities, by their position, and by their sheer size.

Trajan's great octagonal port basin at Portus, still visible today, helped secure food supplies for Rome – in particular the crucial flow of corn from Egypt – and complemented his promotion of the *alimenta* system, which provided food and education for poor and orphaned children across Italy. To the considerable kudos from these initiatives he added his military prowess, and as a result of his achievements the Senate acclaimed him as *optimus princeps* (greatest ruler). Every emperor who followed was exhorted by the Senate to be '*Felicior Augusto, melior Traiano*' – more blessed than Augustus and more righteous than Trajan.

'A MONUMENT UNIQUE UNDER HEAVEN AND ADMIRED BY ALL OF THE GODS'

AMMIANUS
MARCELLINUS

Below: Aerial view reconstruction of the Forum of Trajan, the last and the grandest imperial forum. The Basilica Ulpia (left) looks over the massive colonnaded piazza, while behind the Basilica is Trajan's Column. Beyond the Forum (top right) is the complex of shops, offices and workshops known as Trajan's markets.

Overleaf: A reconstruction of the main piazza of the Forum, looking down from the viewing gallery on the Basilica Ulpia. The piazza, paved with white marble, is surrounded by colonnades, festooned with sculptures of victorious generals and conquered enemies. Before the monumental entrance stands a mounted statue of Trajan, one of the largest in Rome.

Trajan next turned to his monumental legacy within Rome and embarked on building the **FORUM OF TRAJAN**. This last, great imperial forum commemorated Trajan's conquest of Dacia (Romania) and immediately stood out – even among the glories of imperial Rome. Some 250 years later the writer Ammianus Marcellinus called it 'a monument unique under heaven and admired by all of the gods'. This massive complex (at 300 × 180 m, or 984 × 591 ft, twice the size of Augustus's Forum) comprised an immense colonnaded piazza of 200 × 120 m (656 × 394 ft), with an enormous bronze equestrian statue of Trajan; the magnificent Basilica Ulpia; and the Column of Trajan, flanked by libraries. A Temple of the Deified Trajan was almost certainly there, too, while behind the Forum were Trajan's markets, an enormous commercial and administrative centre.

The Forum was parachuted into an area already filled with other structures, and a great natural spur, the junction of the Capitoline and Quirinal Hills. Trajan's architect, Apollodorus of Damascus, had to prepare the whole area, rerouting roads, demolishing structures, reconstructing others (including the Forum of Julius Caesar) and removing the Capitoline/Quirinal spur – all 30 m (98 ft) of it. Dominating the northern side of the piazza was the Basilica Ulpia, named after Trajan's family,

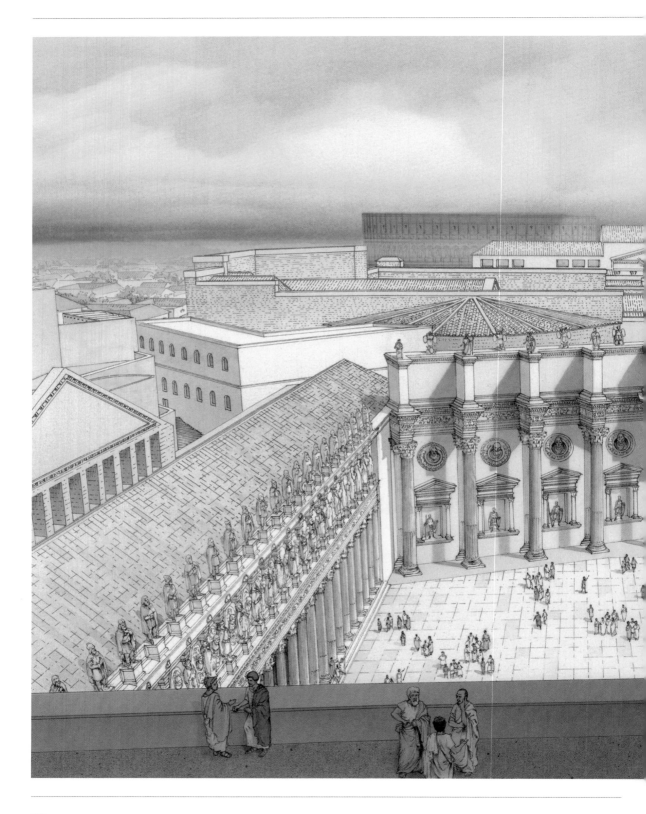

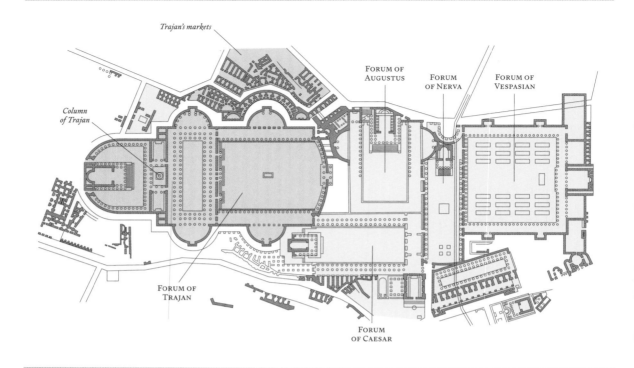

Trajan's markets

Column
of Trajan

FORUM OF
AUGUSTUS

FORUM
OF NERVA

FORUM OF
VESPASIAN

FORUM OF
TRAJAN

FORUM
OF CAESAR

which measured 176 × 60 m (577 × 197 ft) with five aisles and
a ceiling some 25 m (82 ft) high. Many of its columns were of
rare grey granite from Mons Claudianus in central Egypt, while
at the ends of the Basilica were *exedrae* (apses) for law-giving,
a primary function of the Basilica. The piazza, larger than
nearby Piazza Venezia, was paved with around 3,000 thick slabs
of marble (two have survived). As far as the eye could see there
were vast colonnades, the upper storey filled with sculptures
of Dacian prisoners, and great roundels of emperors, and even
exotic animals. Other sculptures, of generals, heroes and the
imperial family, filled the lower storey. As in Augustus's Forum,
the piazza featured a great apsidal *exedra* on both the east and
the west side colonnades. Originally two storeys high, these
were crammed with statuary and coloured marble decoration.
In the centre of the piazza stood a colossal bronze equestrian
statue of Trajan, one of the largest and finest sculptures in
Rome and, at around 10 m (33 ft) tall, three times the size
of the statue of Marcus Aurelius in the Capitoline Museums.

The most prominent element now (though less visible in
antiquity because of surrounding structures) is Trajan's Column.
Made of white, north Italian marble, it is 30 m (98 ft) high, on a
base 8 m (26 ft) high, and originally carried a 5 m-tall (over 16 ft)

Above: A plan of the imperial
forums. These vastly expanded
Rome's commercial and
administrative capacity and
also created a massive new
monumental and metropolitan
quarter. Citizens passed from
one to another, feeling their
different atmospheres and
marvelling at the emperors
who had created them.

Opposite: Trajan's Column
was a tourist attraction even in
antiquity – with an observation
platform reached by an internal
staircase. It is covered with
a spiral frieze, recording the
conquest of Dacia (Romania),
and it also marked the height
of the hill removed to build
Trajan's Forum.

ROME IN GLORY

bronze statue of Trajan. In a very modern touch, an internal staircase leads to a platform giving views over much of the city. The Column's spiral frieze shows Trajan's wars in Dacia in the early AD 100s. The frieze is 190 m (625 ft) long, and has over 2,500 half-size figures of Romans and Dacians fighting, marching, fleeing, begging and dying. This is all shown in continuous narrative, so Trajan features over fifty times. Shown in great detail are Roman and Dacian structures (camps, bridges, huts) and clothing, military equipment and manoeuvres, including the *testudo* ('tortoise') – in which legionaries locked their shields above and around them, like a modern tank. The details were clearer than nowadays, as the figures were freshly carved and probably gloriously painted and gilded.

The base of the Column is covered with depictions of captured Dacian weapons and armour. The inscription says it was erected by the public in gratitude to Trajan (and to show the height of the levelled spur). It also served as the tomb for Trajan and his wife Plotina. The Column was soon followed by two more – of Antoninus Pius and Marcus Aurelius – and it inspired many later monuments such as Napoleon's column in the Place de Vendôme in Paris. It is possible (experts cannot agree) that beyond the Column stood the Temple of the Deified Trajan. One grey granite column found nearby is massive: 18 m (59 ft) tall, it is 3 m (nearly 10 ft) higher than those of the Pantheon.

The Column's detailed frieze provides some of the most important evidence for the Roman army, from military equipment to structures and manoeuvres. In the scene in the left-hand image, Roman legionaries besiege a Dacian settlement, linking their shields in a protective *testudo* (tortoise) formation. On the right, supply boats cross the Danube, while above the emperor addresses his soldiers as supreme commander or *imperator*.

MARBLE IN ROME

ROME IS FULL of marble, but it wasn't always so. The city's local stone is mostly volcanic tufa or travertine (workaday limestone), and all marble was imported. The first marble temple wasn't built until the 140s BC, but thereafter grand building schemes fuelled by Greek influence (and wealth) rapidly covered Rome in marble.

Imperial buildings outwardly gleamed with brilliant white marble from Carrara (northern Italy), Athens and the Greek islands of Paros, Thasos and Proconnesos (now Marmara, Turkey). But their interiors – floors, veneers and columns – glowed with polychrome marbles: honeyed yellow Numidian (Algeria), deep green Thessalian (northern Greece), deep red Spartan (southern Greece), variegated purple and white Phrygian (central Turkey), and green Carystian from the Greek island of Euboea, nicknamed *cipollino* (little onion) for its layered, rippled texture. The conquest of Egypt brought pink and grey granite and prestigious deep red porphyry, an imperial monopoly, which later passed from Rome to Constantinople.

Monuments showed the emperors' power, and so did fine marbles – beautiful, expensive – coming from all over the world that Rome controlled. Thousands worked to quarry, transport and warehouse stone, and many more to carve it and build with it. No efforts were spared. Porphyry, for example, came from just one quarry on a mountainside in Egypt. After Empire, some marble was burned for lime to make cement, or was ground up to make plaster, but much of it was reused. The intricate floors of Rome's medieval churches are made of hacked Roman wall veneer and paving. Even columns of granite and porphyry were reused – sliced into neat circles like a sausage.

The other major surviving element of the Forum is the huge market complex. The orange-pink brick structures, with ornate brick façades, were, it seems, unusually not covered in stucco or brightly painted, but in any case were hidden from the piazza by the Forum's high fire-screen wall. Behind this was a rerouted road, showing the Forum's impact on this busy area. The markets sit on five terraces, linked by a series of covered galleries and passageways, with a two-storeyed 'Great Hall', soaring upward to a vaulted ceiling and filled with doorways and passageways to other areas. An ancient Roman shopping mall? Perhaps in part, but more likely also the administrative hub of the whole Forum complex.

The Forum of Trajan was a wonder of Rome – a spectacular backdrop to important, space-hungry events. Trajan used it for *congiaria* – distributions of money or provisions such as oil and wine to the people. In AD 118 Hadrian marked his accession by very publicly burning all accounts of public debt (900 million

Left: The Via Biberatica, one of the streets that passed through the multistorey expanse of Trajan's markets. Restored in the 1930s, it presents a very atmospheric urban landscape, lined with the wide-open frontages of shops and workshops. Rome was a metropolis of over a million people and retail was everywhere.

Opposite: A reconstruction of the building of the Castello delle Milizie (Castle of the Militias) above the markets. The castle, whose tower still stands, was built in the 1200s by the Conti di Segni family. Each of Rome's warring medieval families had their castles, usually built into ancient monuments.

sesterces – an enormous amount) in the Forum piazza. To make sure it was appreciated, Hadrian issued coins citing the exact value of the debt. Later, Marcus Aurelius was so desperate for money to fund his German wars, he turned Trajan's Forum into a gigantic auction house for imperial property (some of it Hadrian's), including clothing, gold plate and jewelry. In AD 357 the Christian emperor Constantius II, normally resident in Constantinople (modern Istanbul), visited Rome and toured its monuments. When he entered Trajan's Forum he was thunderstruck. He saw Trajan's equestrian statue and said how much he wanted one at Constantinople. 'Your majesty', replied Ormisda, a Persian prince in his court, '...before you can have a horse like that, you must have a stable like this.'

The Forum was maintained and used for centuries, with statue dedications (an indicator of a monument's vitality) continuing well into the 5th century. A French priest tells of readings of Virgil's poetry in the 7th century AD. So the monument, and the memory of Trajan, lived on, sometimes in unexpected quarters. Trajan was acclaimed *optimus princeps* (greatest ruler), by the Senate, but later he was held in great esteem by Christians, as shown in a story about Pope Gregory the Great. Around AD 600 Gregory passed through Trajan's Forum and saw, he believed, a relief of Trajan showing kindness to a grieving woman. Intensely moved, he pleaded with God to save Trajan's immortal soul. God agreed, but warned the Pope never to intercede for a pagan again. Later, Trajan was the only pagan emperor included in Dante Alighieri's *Purgatorio* and *Paradiso*.

Trajan thus became immortal, but his Forum was not. In the AD 660s, the Byzantine emperor Constans II removed the finest sculptures (probably of bronze) and around AD 800 a major earthquake caused widespread damage. Two centuries later, lime-kilns were well established and the major destruction had begun. Today Trajan's Column stands defiantly over the ruins, yet in the 1160s it was almost demolished, saved only by an emergency decree of the medieval Senate. From 1588 St Peter has looked out from the top. During works to set him up, the emperor's bronze feet and head were discovered, but sadly subsequently disappeared.

The great markets are now the major surviving elements of Trajan's Forum, but in antiquity a great fire wall rendered the markets far less visible from the Forum proper. Echoing their varied Roman use, in the Middle Ages houses, a castle and a monastery were all built into the ruins.

Overleaf: A reconstruction of the Circus Maximus, the largest venue for chariot racing (or any form of entertainment) in the Empire. As chariots thundered through seven laps, the roar of the crowd – perhaps 150,000 strong – could be heard for many miles.

The markets, heavily reconstructed in the 1930s, are still labyrinthine and atmospheric, and now house important architecture and sculpture from excavations of the imperial forums. Above them rises the 13th-century Torre delle Milizie (Tower of the Militias), part of the remains of a small castle that occupied the markets' upper levels in the Middle Ages.

As for the glorious Basilica Ulpia, excavations in the early 19th century revealed its full width but less than half its length. Some of its columns have been re-erected, the second tier in 2022, and some scraps of its marble flooring and veneer remain. Of the Forum's enormous quantity of sculptures fewer than twenty fairly complete pieces have been found. Littered everywhere are shapeless, battered, barely recognizable elements of statues, reliefs and columns, with tell-tale marks of chisels used to break the marble into small pieces to burn in the kilns.

Until the 1930s this whole area looked very different, the Forum and its surroundings submerged in the medieval and Renaissance houses of a suburb centred on the Via Alessandrina. Then in the 1930s work began on the Via dell'Impero, later renamed Via dei Fori Imperiali, and the entire suburb was levelled. This revealed much of the Forum and, following further excavations, most of the piazza can be seen, with the rectangular imprints of the great marble slabs and the base of Trajan's colossal statue. One area preserves remains of houses swept away in the 1930s – their cellars, truncated walls and patterned tiles, now a part of Rome's history of ruins.

For Rome the provision of spectacular entertainments was paramount. Juvenal famously commented Romans wanted only 'bread and circuses (*panem et circenses*)', and the emperors had to provide this – very visibly. Trajan's new port at Portus ensured the supply of corn for bread and, as for a circus, he completely rebuilt the mighty CIRCUS MAXIMUS.

The first fixed structures were probably built around 600 BC by King Tarquinius Priscus. In legend, chariot racing began here with Rome's founder and first king, Romulus. He is said to have used chariot races to lure a local tribe, the Sabines, into Rome and take their women for his growing city. Chariot racing was always viewed as the 'senior service' of entertainments, because of its links to Rome's origins and religion.

Filling the valley between the Aventine and Palatine Hills, the Circus Maximus was the largest structure for spectacular entertainment in the ancient world. In Trajan's final form it was 600 m (close to 2,000 ft) long, 180 m (over 590 ft) wide and seated around 200,000 spectators (almost four times the

capacity of the Colosseum) on more than 30 km (18½ miles) of seating. Truly a wonder of the world. Its arcaded exterior, studded with sculptures, stretched as far as the eye could see. The sight of this great façade underlined Rome's power and gave a real sense of civic pride and of being part of *romanitas* ('Romanness').

Seating and structure were originally of wood, and though Julius Caesar rebuilt the lower storey in stone in the 40s BC, the risk of fire remained. Several major fires began in and around the Circus, including the Great Fire of Nero in AD 64. Trajan rebuilt the exterior completely in stone, but the upper seating remained of wood, which collapsed in the AD 290s, with the loss of thousands of lives.

Running down the middle of the Circus was the central reserve or *spina* (literally spine or backbone). The *spina* and the floor of the Circus are now 8 m (26 ft) below ground, but

Part of a mosaic from Piazza Armerina, Sicily, showing a victorious charioteer in his *quadriga* (four-horse chariot). This charioteer belongs to the green team (the others were red, white and blue); these aroused strong feelings of loyalty, and rivalry, among their fans. Here he raises his whip in a sign of victory.

THE CROWD SURGES 'TO AND FRO, WITH A NOISE LIKE THE SOUND OF THE SEA'

SILIUS ITALICUS

its appearance is preserved in art such as the chariot mosaics in Piazza Armerina, Sicily, and Lyons, France. It was crammed with shrines to deities including Venus and Victory, obelisks and other monuments, and at each end of the *spina* were mechanisms to mark the seven laps of the race: sets of bronze eggs were lowered and dolphins tipped. The *spina* was dominated by a 24 m-high (79 ft) obelisk (now in Piazza del Popolo) of Ramesses II, brought from Egypt by Augustus. The emperor Constantius II outdid this in AD 357 with the 32 m-high (105 ft) obelisk of Thutmose III (now in Piazza San Giovanni in Laterano), today the tallest and oldest surviving obelisk outside Egypt. Their age, and the culture and power of Egypt they represented (now transferred to Rome), made them very symbolic.

Just below the imperial palace, Augustus had built the *pulvinar*, literally meaning a 'cushioned seat', but here an ornate shrine for all the statues of the gods involved in the *pompa circensis*, the race-day procession from the Temple of Jupiter on the Capitoline Hill. It was also a grandstand for the emperor and his kin – a clear link between the gods and the imperial family. Embellishing the *pompa*, Titus added a monumental arch at the northern, rounded end of the Circus, through which the parade, and very likely imperial triumphs, would pass.

The Circus Maximus, unlike the Colosseum, had little hierarchy of seating. There was the *pulvinar* or imperial box (albeit shared with the gods!) and probably some reserved seating for senators and VIPs, but otherwise the crowd was not segregated. Juvenal remarked 'All Rome is today at the circus' – and Italy and much of the Empire, too, a great diverse polyglot mass of people. Silius Italicus remarked on the sound of the crowd 'surging to and fro, with a noise like the sound of the sea'. Men and women sat together, and Ovid portrays the Circus as a wonderful place to meet women. His advice? Find out her favourite team and back it, cheer loudly when the statue of Venus goes by in the *pompa*, brush dust from her robe (even if not dusty), and protect her from other people's bony knees. Less romantically, prostitutes plied their trade around the Circus, lending fuel to the Roman authors who were disparaging about the Circus crowd – spending all day at the venue, up to no good and gambling!

From its early history the Circus hosted not only chariot races but also spectacles, such as the *ludi romani* (Roman games) in honour of Jupiter, with military parades and other contests. Before the Colosseum, the Circus was the venue for animal

hunts, too. When Pompey dedicated his Theatre and Temple in 55 BC, he displayed twenty elephants in the Circus, intending them to be hunted and killed. All backfired when the elephants tried to break out of their enclosure into the seating (causing mayhem in the crowd), and then trumpeted pitifully. The crowd turned completely against Pompey – sponsorship came with risks. Julius Caesar (perhaps learning from Pompey's elephant experience) built a broad deep-water channel, or *euripus*, to protect spectators from the beasts. The Circus remained the preferred venue for momentous state occasions. In AD 204, to celebrate the *ludi saeculares* – Rome's centenary games – the emperor Septimius transformed the central *spina* into a massive ship. At the sound of trumpets it disintegrated, disgorging

The Circus Maximus was rebuilt by Trajan almost entirely in stone. After Empire it was intensively quarried, and this view shows just how completely it disappeared, with only some brick-and-concrete arcading and seat foundations surviving. The stadium floor lies 8 m (26 ft) down, buried under silt. Rivers even flowed over the site: the small tower (bottom right) was part of a medieval water mill.

hundreds of wild and exotic animals, including lions, leopards, bears, ostriches – all, of course, were slaughtered.

At the flat end of the Circus were twelve starting gates or *carceres* (literally prison cells) for chariot racing, above which was a VIP box. Here sat a magistrate, who started the race by dropping a white *mappa* or napkin. Through a system of pulleys and cords, all the gates sprang open simultaneously and the chariots raced anti-clockwise for seven laps, covering around 5 km (3 miles). Numbers of races varied. Ten a day was normal, but Domitian (reducing the number of laps to five) supposedly ran a hundred races in a day.

Charioteers, like gladiators, were celebrities. Though low in status (most were slaves or freedmen), they stood extremely high in public regard. The charioteers wore red, white, blue and green, and so did their fans. Obsessive, passionate support for charioteers was known – one fan of the charioteer Felix threw himself on his idol's funeral pyre. Pliny read it in the *Acta diurna* – Rome's daily 'newspaper'. Charioteers were front-page news. The most popular and profitable races involved the four-horse chariot or *quadriga*, which appears often in Roman art. Prize money was huge, but so were the risks, and crashes or *naufragia* – literally 'shipwrecks' – were common. Charioteers wrapped the reins tightly round their waists to control the horses (and always carried a sharp knife to cut the reins and jump clear). The skilled – and lucky – could make a fortune, like the Spanish charioteer Gaius Appuleius Diocles, who retired at forty-two in the early 2nd century AD. He competed in over 4,000 races and amassed a fortune of over 36 million *sesterces* – more money than many of Rome's senators possessed. The best horses came from Spain, Sicily and North Africa, and one of his (Spanish?) horses was a 200-time winner.

Chariot racing remained popular until the end of the Empire. A visitor from southern France in AD 416 said the roar of the crowd could be heard 10 miles (16 km) away. The last recorded chariot race was held in AD 549. Rome's population was now plummeting and the social structure for such spectacles was disappearing. After Empire the Circus was thoroughly quarried. Only scraps remain, a small section of the substructure for the seating at the east (round) end, and battered fragments of Titus's triumphal Arch. The surviving medieval tower was once a water mill, one of many that filled the area when streams returned to the valley, where they had flowed before it was monumentalized.

HADRIAN

(R. AD 117–38)

HADRIAN CAME TO the throne through his adoption by Trajan, just as Trajan had been adopted by his predecessor Nerva. Adoption became the imperial norm throughout the 2nd century AD, enabling the accession of emperors such as Antoninus Pius and Marcus Aurelius. Hadrian spent half his reign travelling around the Empire, partly to see it at first hand, but principally to firm up Rome's frontiers, by creating defences such as Hadrian's Wall in Britain, and by bolstering the morale of the army, which adored him. Wherever he went, he built – from great monuments in places such as Italica in Spain, London in England and Athens in Greece, to whole towns such as Cyrene in Libya. He was very fond of the Greek east, its language and culture, and even wore a Greek-style beard, the first emperor to do so. Some people thought he was perhaps too pro-Greek and called him Graeculus, 'that little Greek', though never to his face.

It was in Rome that Hadrian left his greatest mark, building or completing an array of splendid structures including: the Pantheon; the immense Temple of Venus and Roma; his own mausoleum, now the Castel Sant'Angelo; and the gorgeous Villa Adriana outside Rome at Tivoli. A large, vaulted building, perhaps the culture-loving Hadrian's Athenaeum (used for lectures and recitals) was discovered in Piazza Venezia in 2010 during works for Rome's Metro system. But this emperor was practical, too. He oversaw the construction of swathes of *insulae* (tenement blocks) for Rome's burgeoning population. Hadrian was a fiercely passionate, competitive and intelligent man, and was likely as passionate (and volatile) about architecture as about every other area of his life. He himself may even have had a hand in designing many of the important buildings erected during

PASSIONATE ABOUT ARCHITECTURE, WHEREVER HADRIAN WENT HE BUILT. AND IN ROME HE LEFT HIS GREATEST MARK

The remains of a tenement block (*insula*) abutting the Capitoline Hill, one of many built throughout the city for Rome's growing population during Hadrian's reign. This example originally had six floors with shops at street level, finer accommodation on the lower floors and cheap flats above. Some tenements had as many as eight or nine storeys.

his reign. This passion brought him into conflict with his father's court architect Apollodorus of Damascus.

Hadrian's reign didn't produce only grand buildings. At the base of the Capitoline Hill, under the sweeping staircase leading up to Santa Maria in Aracoeli, are the remains of a Roman *insula*, also known as a **Tenement Building**. Dating to the early to mid-2nd century AD, it was originally at least six storeys high: the modern street level corresponds to the third floor. On the Roman ground level are the large square entrances of *tabernae* (shops and bars), with arched windows and balconies of well-appointed apartments on the second and third floors. Poorer accommodation and single rooms occupied the upper two levels.

Insulae were home to most of the inhabitants of Rome and other major cities of the Empire – a 4th-century AD census of Rome's monuments records over 45,000 of them. Whole sections of the city, such as the Subura slums north of the imperial forums, were composed of *insulae*, but they were not limited to such areas, and were even built right next to important monuments, as here at the Capitoline Hill. Hadrian laid out a large area of *insulae* in the north of the city, along the Via Lata (Via del Corso), but not

all *insulae* were as well planned or thought out. Many were poorly built, causing frequent collapses; others were breeding grounds for disease; and all were potential death traps because of fire. Some were clearly worryingly high – Augustus had legislated against *insulae* more than 21 m (70 ft) tall (eight or nine storeys). The comic writer Martial describes a 'parasite' or dinner scrounger trudging up the 200 steps to his top-floor apartment.

Part of this Capitoline *insula* was occupied into late antiquity, and the building was altered to take into account rising road levels. In fact all other known *insulae* in Rome are now below modern ground level, often forming the foundations for later structures, especially churches, such as the multi-layered San Clemente al Laterano. This one survived through its partial conversion into a church in the 12th/13th century AD. The surviving frescoes and the bell tower are from that early church and, like the tenement itself, were exposed only when the surrounding area of densely packed housing – in character similar to the ancient tenements – was demolished in the 1930s.

In AD 135, only a few years before he died, Hadrian was able to dedicate his greatest monument, the **TEMPLE OF VENUS AND ROMA**. Venus, as the Roman people's protector and founder, had an extremely important place – as seen in Julius Caesar's Temple of Venus Genetrix in his Forum. But this was the first temple to worship Roma as the embodiment of the city – its essence and spirit – paralleling the worship of the emperor's spirit (though not himself), through the imperial cult. This was something new for Rome, unique in layout and the largest and finest temple in the city.

Having cleared the site, which involved shifting (with a squad of twenty-four elephants) the Colossus of Nero to its final position near the Colosseum, Hadrian and Apollodorus of Damascus, the architect he had inherited from Trajan, set to work. Hadrian himself is said to have played a role in drawing up the plans. Perhaps reflecting his love of all aspects of Greek culture, this massive temple was very Greek in style: 'peripteral' (i.e. with columns all around), with a double row of columns down the sides and three rows at the front. Uniquely, it housed two *cellae* (sacred spaces) back to back, with Venus facing the Colosseum and Roma the Forum. The Temple stood on an immense colonnaded platform some 100 × 150 m (330 × 490 ft), as large as the Forum of Augustus, and perhaps intended to have the same functions – making it, in effect, the last of the imperial forums. With its massive presence and its roof of gilded bronze, the Temple was a wonder of the city.

Opposite: The remains of Hadrian's Temple of Venus and Roma, now partly occupied by the church of Santa Francesca Romana. The Temple was built on the site of part of the Domus Aurea, where Nero's bronze Colossus still stood. Hadrian had it relocated using twenty-four elephants. Today only the brick and concrete *cellae* and re-erected granite and porphyry columns remain of the largest temple in Rome.

If the Temple was beautiful and harmonious, the relationship between its creators was not. During Trajan's reign Apollodorus had suggested Hadrian didn't understand architecture and should 'stick to his gourds' (possibly a jibe at Hadrian's interest in organic-shaped domes). Now, Apollodorus rashly criticized him over the proportions of the Temple's *cellae*, quipping that the gigantic cult statues of the goddesses would be unable to get out of these ill-proportioned spaces. Only then, perhaps, did he finally realize the depth of Hadrian's passion for architecture and the limits of his temper, because the emperor had him banished and (some believed) put to death.

Destroyed by fire in the AD 290s, the Temple was rebuilt by the last great pagan emperor, Maxentius, in the early 4th century, and it is the remains of his structure that can be seen today. It survived intact until AD 630, when Pope Honorius took its gilded tiles to use in St Peter's Basilica. The building then rapidly deteriorated, and by the 8th century it housed, on the Forum side, a church to St Peter and St Paul (the patrons of Rome), now Santa Francesca Romana. The foundations of the church, uncovered in the 19th century, comprised thousands of pieces of worked marble from the Temple. Further, massive

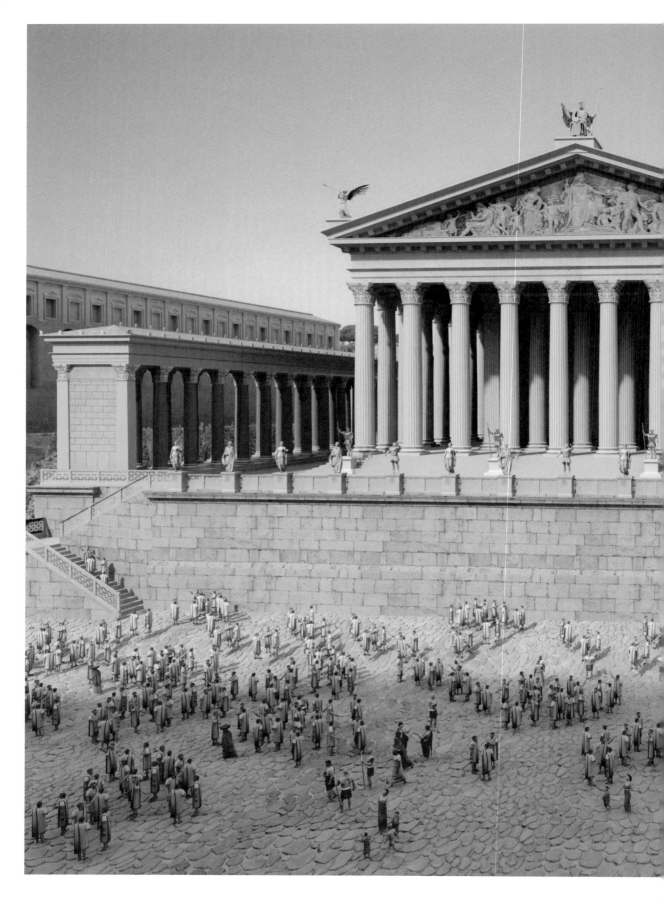

damage was caused in the 1450s when most of the Temple
was thoroughly quarried.

The western *cella* facing onto the Forum, which housed
Roma, somehow survived and is particularly well preserved.
Slightly less so (though visitable) is the *cella* of Venus, facing
the Colosseum. Its ornate lozenge vault decoration, the
alternating niches on the wall and the battered columns of red
granite are faint echoes of the original rich decoration. Outside,
a forest of marble columns 15 m (49 ft) high, long ago reused
or burnt to lime, once towered over the bustling piazza of
the Colosseum. After restoration work in the 1930s, the place
of each column was represented by bushes or small trees.
In 2007 the Italian fashion designer Valentino gained permission
to rebuild many of the columns temporarily in fibreglass for
a grand celebratory dinner, culminating with fireworks against
the backdrop of the Colosseum. In 2021 the Temple was restored
by another famous fashion house, Fendi. Both are examples of
how the ancient monuments retain their fascination and kudos,
even in ruin – an emperor would be proud.

The **PANTHEON** is one of the best-preserved buildings from
Classical antiquity, and its scale, stunning interior and graceful
strength have earned it a special place in the hearts and minds
of visitors to Rome. Michelangelo thought the Pantheon
was '*disegno angelico e non umano*' (a design of angels not men),
while Henry James called it 'by far the most beautiful piece
of ancientry in Rome....The very delicacy of grandeur'.

The Pantheon is for many the most remarkable building
in Rome, but it is also one of the most enigmatic. Fundamental

questions remain around when and by whom it was really built and most importantly, what it was for. The name probably derives from the Greek *pan* 'all' and *theon* 'of the gods', suggesting it was a temple, though a slightly different reading, less strictly religious, is 'all revered'. In fact, there is no *cella* inside the building, and outside no trace of an altar, the usual focus of pagan worship. The Pantheon's few Roman mentions focus on meetings between emperors and Senate and the reading of imperial decrees. It is very possible the Pantheon was for the cult of the emperor and the imperial family – the glue of the Empire.

Hadrian dedicated 'his' Pantheon in around AD 125, yet it is his predecessor Trajan's brick stamps that appear throughout the building. Once set on a high podium, dominating a great rectangular colonnaded square, this Pantheon replaced the original dedicated by Agrippa in 25 BC, twice destroyed by fire. Hadrian demonstrated his respect for Rome's past by putting

CONCRETE

AUGUSTUS SUPPOSEDLY claimed he found Rome brick and left it marble. Perhaps, but behind it all was concrete (*opus caementicium*), strictly a mortared rubble but universally known as concrete. All the great imperial buildings, from baths to basilicas, theatres to arenas, and the great walls that encompassed them, were dependent on it. It comprised an aggregate (hard core), a binder and water. The aggregate used pieces of stone, brick, tile and even amphora fragments, though for vaults and roofs the much lighter pumice was preferred. The binding agent contained quicklime, obtained from burning limestone or marble,

and the key ingredient – volcanic pozzolana dust. This could be found near Rome, but the finest quality pozzolana was imported from the Bay of Naples.

Adding pozzolana produced an extremely strong mortar, which carried on hardening and strengthening for some time. Very importantly, the chemical reaction between pozzolana, quicklime and sea water allowed Roman concrete to set even underwater, making it perfect for harbour works, marine villas and even fish farms, in coastal cities all over the Empire.

Roman concrete wasn't poured, but layered, or assembled and placed

in blocks. Wooden shuttering was used for foundations, while for the walls, brick or stone facings were put in place and then infilled with layers of concrete. Vaults and arches rose on great wooden moulds and frames. The lightness and strength of concrete made possible the construction of the Colosseum and many other monuments, which, if built only of masonry, would have collapsed under their own weight. It also allowed breathtaking architecture such as the magnificent dome of the Pantheon to soar, unsupported – all thanks to humble concrete.

Agrippa's name on the front (but then, perhaps, it wasn't his to name...). It is made up of three seemingly mismatched elements – the large, domed rotunda, the colonnaded porch and a rather boxy junction block. But brick stamps indicate they are contemporary and were planned together.

The great curved brick and concrete walls of the rotunda are 6 m (nearly 20 ft) thick, with integrated arches and piers and great internal voids, which together strengthen the structure by distributing the weight load and channelling the thrust from the upper wall and the dome. The rotunda walls were once covered with plaster, to resemble marble veneer, but in the porch they were sheathed in thick Pentelic marble from Athens. There were already round buildings in Rome, such as the Temple of Vesta, but a round public building of the Pantheon's scale was truly unusual. Together with the great rotunda of Augustus's Mausoleum at the other end of the Campus Martius, the Pantheon was architecturally revolutionary.

The Pantheon still preserves much of its original internal decoration. Great columns of North African marble support the architrave, while marbles from Turkey, Greece and Egypt decorate walls and floor. The columned shrines now hold Christian saints rather than emperors or pagan gods. This great central apse originally held statues of Venus, Mars and the deified Julius Caesar.

The porch columns are granite monoliths 12 m (over 39 ft) high, weighing around 60 tons each, all imported from Egypt, with Aswan red granite shafts at the back and, at the front, rarer, more prestigious, grey granite columns from Mons Claudianus. From there, huge blocks of granite were loaded onto enormous sixteen-wheeler ox-carts and taken to the Nile to be transported to the sea and thence to Rome. It is staggering to think of these huge columns going through the narrow, crowded streets of the city.

The doorway, with its massive, ancient bronze doors and surround, was flanked by colossal statues of Agrippa and Augustus (who piously turned down a statue inside the building). The pediment was too shallow for statues, so was probably covered with decorated sheet bronze, perhaps showing an imperial eagle, recalling the eagle that landed on the Pantheon's pediment before the death and deification of Augustus.

Roman writers give an idea of the appearance of the original Pantheon. Inside, the largest niche (now the apse, containing the icon of the Madonna) housed a statue of the deified Julius Caesar,

'SIMPLE, ERECT, SEVERE, AUSTERE, SUBLIME – SHRINE OF ALL SAINTS AND TEMPLE OF ALL GODS, FROM JOVE TO JESUS – SPARED AND BLEST BY TIME'

LORD BYRON,
Childe Harold's Pilgrimage

Opposite: The Pantheon's dome was the world's largest until the 20th century. Its height is the same as its greatest width, creating a perfect sphere. Add to this the elegant coffering and the ingenious opening or *oculus*, letting in light, and we truly arrive at Shelley's 'unmeasured dome of Heaven'.

Right: A view of the Pantheon seen through neighbouring buildings. Like many imperial monuments, it originally sat at the end of a colonnaded piazza. This vanished during the Middle Ages and it assumed its current setting.

accompanied by Venus and Mars. Significantly, Venus's statue wore earrings made from one of Queen Cleopatra's expensive pearls. Cleopatra was submitting to Venus – and to Rome. The Pantheon was as much about statecraft as about religion.

Septimius Severus restored the Pantheon in the AD 200s, in its Hadrianic form (while putting his own name firmly on the pediment). The interior preserves original decoration, including much of the floor with its classic pattern of squares and circles of coloured marble, many columns and pilasters, the wall veneer and some of the columned shrines or *loculi* (literally, niches). The band of decoration below the dome (partly recreated in the 1930s), with its grille windows and pilasters, was intact until 1747 when Pope Benedict XIV and his architect Piranesi ripped the 'unsatisfactory' scheme out. The generally good state of repair shows how other buildings could have survived, without the pillaging of the Middle Ages and Renaissance.

The most stunning feature of the Pantheon is the dome, soaring to over 43.3 m (142 ft) above the visitor. It is so tall that Trajan's Column, complete with its statue of St Peter, could stand at the centre of the floor and not touch the top, while the Statue of Liberty without its podium is only 3 m (10 ft) taller. Seen from outside, the dome seems flatter and springs from relatively high up (but it would nevertheless have looked stunning with its roof of gilded bronze tiles). Inside, very cleverly, the dome springs much lower down; in fact the dome's diameter is the same as its height, creating the appearance of a perfect sphere of harmony and balance.

Veduta della Piazza della Rotonda

This breathtaking vault, the largest dome anywhere until the 20th century, and still the world's largest unreinforced dome, was possible only because of concrete, and the use of different densities and weights of concrete was key. The lowest part uses a heavier aggregate of crushed brick and mortar, while the highest, around the open apex or *oculus* (eye), contains lighter crushed tufa and volcanic slag from the Bay of Naples. The thickness of the concrete varied too, from around 6.5 m (21 ft) at the base of the dome, to just over 1 m (3 ft) at the *oculus*, reducing weight without affecting strength. The coffering panels, arranged in five rows of twenty-eight, reduced weight still further (and were very attractive). They were probably painted deep blue, perhaps with central gilded bronze stars creating, in the poet Shelley's words, 'the unmeasured dome of Heaven'.

The great hole or *oculus*, 8.5 m (28 ft) across, lightened the dome at its weakest point, and also allowed a beam of light to play on the interior. Was the Pantheon, among other things,

A view of the Pantheon and its surroundings in the 1760s by Giovanni Battista Piranesi. The surrounding buildings were more ramshackle than those of today, while the unsurfaced piazza was an open market of shacks and stalls. The Pantheon here still has its bell towers known as the 'asses' ears'.

'A DESIGN OF ANGELS NOT MEN'

MICHELANGELO

a great sundial? Fascinatingly, on 21 April (the legendary birth day of Rome), the beam falls squarely on the great doors – perhaps for the symbolic entry of the emperor? The *oculus* also lets in rain, which drains away through holes in the floor. This ingress of nature has not always been appreciated, and in the 18th century permanent glazing of the *oculus* was discussed. The British nurse Florence Nightingale, who visited in the 1840s during a Mass after a downpour, was not impressed. The reflection of people and candles on the watery floor made her think of the Underworld, with the souls of the dead near the River Styx.

The Pantheon survived partly because of its robust structure, but mainly because, in AD 608, it was given to the Pope by the Eastern emperor Phocas to be converted into a church – first Santa Maria ad Martyres (St Mary and the Martyrs) and then Santa Maria della Rotonda. The Pantheon's status as a church could not protect it completely. In AD 663 its gilded bronze tiles were stripped by the Eastern emperor Constans II. In 1625 Pope Urban VIII took the bronze beams and the beautiful coffered ceiling of the porch – over 204,000 kg (450,000 lbs) of bronze, including 4,080 kg (9,000 lbs) from the nails alone – to be melted down to make cannons for Castel Sant'Angelo. The Pope (of the Barberini family) claimed the bronze was for the *baldacchino* (altar canopy) of St Peter's Basilica, but the people weren't fooled and coined the phrase '*quod non fecerunt barbari, fecerunt Barberini*' (What the barbarians didn't do, the Barberini did).

A more planned structural change involved the addition in the 17th century of twin bell towers, 'the asses' ears'. They were removed in the 1880s, when the popes no longer controlled the city, in what seemed to some an act of provocation to the Church. Also during the 19th century many simple buildings, shops and stalls were cleared from around the monument, though, fortunately, Mussolini's proposals to sweep away any remaining structures and leave the Pantheon in a vast sterile piazza were never realized.

In its sacred capacity the Pantheon also served as a burial place for the wealthy and famous – the composer Arcangelo Corelli, the painter Annibale Carracci and, most famously, the painter, architect and antiquarian Raffaello Sanzio (Raphael). His desire to rest here emphasized the Pantheon's importance, inextricably linked to its ancient Roman origins. It was also appropriate given his role as the pope's prefect (recorder and protector) of Roman Antiquities.

Raphael's tomb was rediscovered in the 1830s. The archaeologist Rodolfo Lanciani, who saw the bones, said Raphael had 'great roughness of the thumb...characteristic of painters'. He was reburied appropriately, in a Roman-style sarcophagus. Some kings and queens of Italy are also buried here, including Victor Emmanuel II, first king of united Italy, in a great bronze casket.

The Pantheon has an enormous legacy, inspiring so many other structures, from the *caldarium* (hot room) of the Baths of Caracalla, to the dome of Hagia Sophia in Istanbul, St Peter's in Rome, St Paul's in London, the Capitol Building in Washington and (thankfully never built) Hitler's 300 m-high (984 ft) Volkshalle in Berlin. In architecture, art and emotion, few monuments come close to the impact of the Pantheon.

The **MAUSOLEUM OF HADRIAN** (now Castel Sant'Angelo) and its bridge, the **PONS AELIUS** (now Ponte Sant'Angelo), were started by Hadrian and completed by his successor Antoninus Pius in AD 139. It was the resting-place for emperors from Hadrian and his wife Sabina, up to Caracalla in AD 217. Even the disgraced Commodus, son of Marcus Aurelius, was accommodated. Septimius Severus was laid to rest here in the burial chest of his idol Marcus Aurelius. Modelled on Augustus's Mausoleum, it comprised a rotunda, over 60 m (197 ft) high and 64 m (210 ft) wide, on a podium about 89 m (292 ft) square. The exterior was covered with white Italian marble and decorated with bronze and marble statues.

In about AD 400 the Mausoleum became a major bastion in Rome's city walls. The historian Procopius gives a dramatic account of its Roman defenders repelling a siege by the Goths in AD 537, by breaking up the Mausoleum's marble statues and hurling them at the attackers. The monument received its present name some sixty years later, when plague was ravaging the city. Pope Gregory the Great saw a vision of the Archangel Michael above the Mausoleum, and as the angel sheathed his sword the plague ceased.

The Mausoleum became the principal stronghold of the popes, connected to St Peter's Basilica by a fortified passageway, the Passetto di Borgo. During the 16th century a suite of suitably fine rooms was created in the upper levels. These were all partly decorated in grotesque style – 'fourth Pompeian style' frescoes, filled with fine and fiddly details, inspired by those being rediscovered in the damp, buried corridors of Nero's palace, the Domus Aurea. The 'Pauline' Hall includes over-life-size fresco depictions of Hadrian and the Archangel Michael, while

The tomb of the Renaissance artist Raphael, rediscovered in 1830, is located under one of the Pantheon's shrines. The Pantheon had particular relevance for Raphael who, as the Pope's prefect of Antiquities, was responsible for protecting what remained of ancient Rome.

Below: Detail of a fresco depicting Hadrian in full Roman military uniform in the Pauline Hall of Castel Sant'Angelo. In the Middle Ages the Mausoleum of Hadrian became the pope's main fortress in Rome and was renamed after the Archangel Michael. The papal rooms were redecorated with such 'grotesque' style frescoes in the 1540s by Pope Paul II.

Overleaf: The Mausoleum of Hadrian (Castel Sant'Angelo), seen from the Aelian bridge (Ponte Sant'Angelo) that connects it to the city, was the resting place for Rome's rulers for one hundred years.

the library has a riot of 'fourth style' paintings on the ceiling and high relief stucco of Classical motifs. Below these apartments was a different face of papal Rome – dungeons, built by Pope Alexander VI for religious criminals and heretics. A private toilet in the first dungeon suggests a hierarchy even in imprisonment.

Connecting the Mausoleum to the main part of the city was the Pons Aelius (named after the family of Hadrian), now Ponte Sant'Angelo, slabbed with basalt, decorated with statues, and fitted with finely carved marble parapets. In the Middle Ages it was the main crossing to reach St Peter's Basilica, but in 1450 there was a stampede among the pilgrims. Hundreds were crushed or drowned and much of the Roman superstructure was destroyed.

A fortress, of course, needed vantage points, and the Mausoleum afforded some of the finest. Arguably the best is from the Terrace of the Archangel, the setting for the dramatic finale of Puccini's opera *Tosca*. On a brighter note, from the 1470s the fortress has been the backdrop to the *Girandola,* literally the Catherine Wheel or Pinwheel. This is a major firework display held on Easter Monday or 28 June, the eve of the feast day of St Peter and St Paul, Rome's patrons. The Mausoleum became in Roman eyes a place of festival

Illustration from the 1780s
of the *Girandola* (literally
Catherine Wheel or Pinwheel),
a massive fireworks display
against the backdrop of the
Mausoleum. At Easter and
in late June on the eve of
the feast day of Rome's
patrons, St Peter and St Paul,
the Mausoleum erupted in
festival and celebration.

and celebration – as can be seen on a myriad depictions of the event throughout the centuries.

Most of the Hadrianic exterior has vanished and the squared base of the Mausoleum – clearly shown in 15th-century drawings, with its decorated masonry facing intact – is now englobed in later building. The rotunda, its marble veneer long gone, reveals its substructure of concrete and green tufa, but much still remains of the internal structure of the Mausoleum. At the entrance a ramp goes down into a squared reception area with a niche, once filled with a colossal statue of Hadrian. A great ramp spirals up to the top of the building, with occasional fragments of original white mosaic. Walking through atmospheric vaulted staircases, the visitor crosses a footbridge passing right over the top of the Sala delle Urne (Room of the Urns). This square chamber is lined with travertine blocks (once marble-veneered) and has a barrel-vaulted stone ceiling originally covered with gilded and painted stucco and mosaic. Here, in three great niches, were the beautiful ash urns of Hadrian and other emperors, including Antoninus Pius and Marcus Aurelius (with his admirer and urn-sharer Septimius Severus). Appropriately, a quote from Hadrian's poetry is displayed on the facing wall, the only surviving fragment of his many works.

> *Animula, vagula, blandula*
> *Hospes comesque corporis*
> *Quae nunc abibis in loca*
> *Pallidula, rigida, nudula,*
> *Nec, ut soles, dabis iocos...*
>
> Ah! gentle, fleeting, wav'ring sprite,
> Friend and associate of this clay!
> To what unknown region borne,
> Wilt thou, now, wing thy distant flight?
>
> No more, with wonted humour gay,
> But pallid, cheerless, and forlorn.

FRAGMENT OF HADRIAN'S POETRY,

translated by GEORGE GORDON, LORD BYRON

HADRIAN'S SUCCESSORS

W HEN HADRIAN DIED at the seaside resort of Baiae, the Empire passed to his adopted successor Antoninus Pius (r. AD 138–61). He was a very safe pair of hands for Hadrian's legacy, but Hadrian also insisted on the simultaneous appointment of Antoninus's successors, the future co-emperors Marcus Aurelius and Lucius Verus, to ensure a period of stability. Antoninus, unlike Hadrian, was not a great military man or traveller, but his piety to his adoptive father, his even temper and fair treatment of all citizens (even the enslaved), gave him his name and earned him his place as one of the 'good emperors' in Rome's 'golden age' of the 2nd century AD. Substantial parts of his two major building projects survive, the Temple of the Deified Hadrian and the Temple of the Deified Faustina.

Near the Pantheon, in the aptly named Piazza di Pietra (Stone Square), is a great wall of masonry and columns, the well-preserved long north side of the **TEMPLE OF THE DEIFIED HADRIAN**, dedicated in AD 145 by Antoninus. By the time of his death, the Senate despised Hadrian for his execution of several aristocrats, supposedly for treason, and was more inclined to damn his memory than glorify it. Antoninus, in a rare display of irritation, threatened to step down. Hadrian was duly deified and this temple was built, in a part of the Campus Martius which had already acquired a strong link with Hadrian, through the Pantheon and a temple to his beloved mother-in-law Matidia. Over the centuries more than two dozen large, sculpted slabs have been found nearby, which probably formed a frieze around the top of the piazza portico. Displayed now in the Capitoline Museums and museums in Rome and Naples, they show military trophies and female personifications of the Empire's provinces.

Opposite: Relief from the piazza of the Temple of the Deified Hadrian, showing the personification of an imperial province. This province, with her military style clothing and cloak, may represent Hispania (Spain).

Above: The left side of the Temple of the Deified Hadrian still stands. The piazza, now below ground level, was surrounded by a colonnade, once decorated with reliefs showing Rome's provinces.

Here, the provinces are not conquered enemies, bound and bowed, but dignified, loyal members of Hadrian's Empire. Peaceful collaboration, not conquest, is the strong message, mirroring Hadrian's mission to knit the Empire tightly together.

When Antoninus died, his adopted heirs Marcus Aurelius, who had grown up in the imperial court, and Lucius Verus, the son of Hadrian's intended successor Aelius Caesar, who died young, took the reins as co-emperors. They worked together effectively and relatively harmoniously, just as well, because pressures were building from the Germanic tribes on the Rhine and Danube and from the Persians in the east, and the Empire was wracked by plague. There was little opportunity to focus on architecture, but two monuments in Rome, linked to the thoughtful and philosophical Marcus Aurelius (r. AD 161–80), capture the power of Empire and emperor: his own equestrian statue, and the so-called Antonine Column.

Dominating the covered courtyard of the Capitoline
Museums is the imposing **EQUESTRIAN STATUE OF THE
EMPEROR MARCUS AURELIUS**, for almost 400 years the focal
point of Michelangelo's piazza on the Capitoline Hill. Outside
in the piazza now is a perfect copy, with the original in a
controlled environment – in stark contrast to the centuries
it stood open to the elements (and human misuse). The statue
shows the emperor, recognizable from many other statues and
busts, in a commanding pose, but not as *imperator* (commander-
in-chief) in full military uniform. Instead, under his military
cloak he wears a plain tunic, while his shoes are aristocratic,
not military. The emperor, like all Roman riders, didn't use
stirrups, which were introduced by barbarians after Rome fell.

His left hand once held a bridle, while his right extends
in a gesture of *adlocutio* or address, perhaps towards the
army or the people in general. Equestrian statues were a Greek
tradition adopted in the Republic by the Romans, along with
many other Greek ideas. It was during the Empire, however,
that the image of the ruler astride his horse, his hand outstretched
in a gesture of imperial authority, became so powerful.

In late antiquity there were over twenty *equi magni* (large
equestrian statues – literally 'big horses') throughout the city,
but this is the only survivor. After the statue's original identity
was forgotten, it was identified variously as Mark Antony and
Septimius Severus. It was the common medieval belief that the
statue was the 'Christian' emperor Constantine that probably
saved it from being melted down like all the others (including,

ironically, the colossal statue of Constantine in the Forum Romanum). No one is sure where the statue was originally set up, but for much of the Middle Ages it stood outside Rome's cathedral of San Giovanni in Laterano. The statue became a popular spot to display the bodies of the pope's enemies – one was even suspended from it by his hair. In 1538 it was moved to the Capitoline Hill (against huge protests from the Lateran clergy) to be the centrepiece of Michelangelo's redesigned piazza.

Horse and rider are remarkably well preserved considering their eventful 1,800-year history, surviving late antiquity and the Middle Ages, transport across Rome and even a forced march to Paris as part of Napoleon's caravan of looted European art. Conservation has revealed techniques of manufacture including the complex twelve-part casting of the horse, and also the effects of prolonged exposure to the elements. A striking amount of gilding remains, though there is inevitable surface corrosion and damage to the interior, through water pooling – and not just water. In the Middle Ages the statue was a focal point for festivals and feasts, and at a celebration in 1348 the horse became a fountain, spouting wine and water from its nostrils.

Following the death of Verus in AD 169, Marcus named his own son, Commodus, as successor, thereby ending the hugely successful eighty-year tradition of adoption. Commodus (r. AD 180–92) proved less capable than his father, and left affairs of state to (generally untrustworthy) courtiers. He hid his mortal shortcomings behind a mask of living divinity, associating himself with the demi-god Hercules, and (to the Senate's disgust) fought in the gladiatorial arena dressed as Hercules. Gripped by increasing paranoia, he launched a major purge of his supposed enemies and finally in AD 192, almost universally hated, he was assassinated. The Senate decreed him to be 'more brutal than Domitian, more vile than Nero...'. With his death, the Antonine dynasty and the 'golden' 2nd century AD ended. Commodus had begun to repair some of the ravages of the terrible fire of AD 191, though this was mostly completed by others. But he personally left one very impressive legacy, a monument to his father – the Temple (now gone) and COLUMN OF MARCUS AURELIUS (the 'Antonine Column').

Looming today over Piazza Colonna and the Via del Corso, the Column was probably dedicated by Commodus in AD 184, and was once part of a complex including an altar and the great temple to the deified Marcus Aurelius and his wife Faustina.

The Column of Marcus Aurelius commemorated his wars on the Rhine and Danube. Like Trajan's Column, it uses continuous narrative, has a viewing platform – and a statue of a saint (Paul) instead of its original emperor. Originally set in a great piazza, and exposed to the elements, it was saved from imminent collapse by the Pope's architect in 1589. He mistakenly inscribed 'Antoninus Pius' on its base, hence its other (incorrect) name, the 'Antonine' Column.

It stands 30 m (98 ft) high on a base originally another 10 m (33 ft) high, once decorated with reliefs of Victories and subjugated barbarians, removed in the 16th century. An internal staircase led up to a panoramic viewing platform, while at the top was a colossal bronze statue of Marcus Aurelius, 6–7 m (20–23 ft) high. This disappeared in the Middle Ages, but was replaced in 1589 by a statue of St Paul, echoing the statue of St Peter set up on Trajan's Column the year before. There was a conscious twinning of the monuments in later history, but the ancient experience of the columns was very different. Trajan's was hemmed in by the Basilica Ulpia and other structures, while that of Marcus Aurelius stood in an open piazza in front of his Temple.

The decoration commemorates Marcus Aurelius's victories over the Quadi and Marcomanni tribes on the Rhine and Danube in the AD 170s. They were the first foreign enemies to invade Italy since Hannibal, 400 years earlier. As on Trajan's Column, the relief is carved in a helix, with Victory dividing the narrative into two military campaigns, and is executed in continuous narrative, featuring the emperor many times. There are generic pictures of military life but also some specific events. Several writers, including Marcus Aurelius, recorded one pictured episode in Moravia (Czech Republic) when, after a severe drought, a violent storm broke. A great bearded figure opens his cloak and unleashes a tempest, drenching the Romans but bombarding the barbarians with large hailstones, blasting them with lightning and drowning them.

A scene on the Column of Marcus Aurelius depicting a dramatic moment from a campaign on the Danube. The Romans were about to engage the enemy when a violent storm descended and blasted the tribes with lightning and huge hailstones. The relief shows a huge winged and bearded storm god opening up his watery cloak. Around him the Romans still stand, but below is a stack of drowned tribesmen and their horses.

The Column of Marcus Aurelius shown in a print of 1589, when it was restored by Domenico Fontana, chief architect to Pope Sixtus V. The print bears Fontana's incorrect identification of *Columna Antonina* (the Antonine Column). But Fontana was not the column's first champion: inscriptions of around AD 190 found nearby in the 1770s mention Adrastus, the Column's original caretaker.

In the relief, perspective is more simply shown: figures, though carved in deeper relief than on Trajan's Column, are fewer, thinned out and appear simply and more frontally. This is moving away from the Classical ideal, hints perhaps of the artistic changes that would become clearer in the 3rd century. Overall, the scenes portrayed and the way in which they are executed give the Column a different feel. The order and process of Trajan's Column, in a sense, give way to the drama and chaos of Marcus Aurelius's.

The Column was immediately a remarkable feature of the city. Monuments needed to be looked after, and inscriptions discovered nearby in the 1770s give a rare insight into this side of monumentality. They concern a *procurator*, or caretaker of the Column, called Adrastus, who was allowed to build a house nearby in order to carry out his duties more efficiently. Clearly, there was a whole army of people throughout the ancient city who guarded, cleaned, swept, and afforded (or barred) entry to Rome's monuments. Two hundred years later in 357 when the emperor Constantius II visited the city, the two columns are mentioned as 'exalted heights with platforms to which one may mount'. In the Middle Ages the Column's viewing platform remained a jealously guarded source of income for the local monastery.

The centuries, however, took their toll. The Column's high relief is badly weathered, especially on the west side, exposed to salt winds from the sea. The whole structure, like other monuments, was severely weakened by removal of its iron clamps, and by the 16th century it was in serious danger of collapse. There were splits of up to 9 m (30 ft) along its length, its internal staircase was impassable, and some elements were displaced by as much as 15 cm (6 in.) through torsion from earthquakes. Fortunately in AD 1589 the Column was restored by the papal architect Domenico Fontana, and the whole structure was stabilized. Missing elements were reintegrated using, sadly, marble from another beautiful monument, the great multi-storeyed Septizodium, which Septimius Severus built as a monumental façade for part of the Palatine Hill. Fontana left an unintentional legacy in his new inscription on the base, misidentifying the emperor commemorated as Antoninus Pius. This idea stuck, giving the monument its usual (incorrect) name, the Antonine Column.

SEPTIMIUS SEVERUS

(R. AD 193–211)

After Commodus's assassination, the Empire was plunged again into civil war. From this chaos (reaching such a point that one emperor, Didius Julianus, bought the Empire at auction from the imperial guards) emerged Septimius Severus. Hailing from Leptis Magna in modern Libya, North Africa, he was an extremely capable general who, backed by his legions from the Danube, seized power in AD 193 and brought the Empire back together. Hailing from North Africa, Severus married a Syrian aristocrat, Julia Domna, and raised his two sons in Rome. He spent much of his reign on campaign, especially in the east (modern Iraq), but died in Britain in AD 211.

Severus was also one of the most prolific imperial builders. When a huge fire in AD 191 devastated Rome's Campus Martius, he rebuilt a whole swathe of monuments including the Pantheon, the Temple of Peace and the Portico of Octavia (always adding his own name somewhere prominent). He also erected his own monuments, including the Arch of Severus, the Temple of Vesta, the Arch of the Bankers (Arco degli Argentarii), and fittingly, the great marble plan of the city (*forma urbis*) on which these and other monuments were shown.

The **Temple of Vesta** was first built, according to legend, by King Numa (715–673 BC) who founded the order of Vestal priestesses, and was last rebuilt around AD 200, probably by Julia Domna who was closely linked to the cult. The battered fragments of her Temple survive today, in a 1930s reconstruction. The Temple, built of white marble, was circular and about 15 m (49 ft) in diameter, similar to the surviving round temple in the Forum Boarium. Inside were two of Rome's greatest treasures: the sacred flame, burning here in the symbolic heart (and hearth)

SEVERUS WAS A SUCCESSFUL GENERAL AND ALSO ONE OF THE MOST PROLIFIC IMPERIAL BUILDERS

Below: Julia Domna, wife and empress of Septimius Severus, shown on a beryl gemstone. Julia Domna was popular in Rome, particularly among the army, for whom she was 'Mother of the Camps'. She was also linked to important cults in the city, in particular the cult of Vesta.

Right: The remains of the Temple of Vesta. It had a round *tholos* form, in Greek style and, at 15 m (49 ft) across, was deceptively large. Tended by the Vestal priestesses, it housed the sacred flame, symbolizing Rome's hearth and its continuity. The smaller, darker elements, set in new travertine, are what remain from the destruction of the monument in 1549.

of the city and ensuring its continuity; and the Palladium, the ancient wooden image of Athena/Minerva, brought by Prince Aeneas from Troy. According to legend, when the Temple burned down in the 240s BC, the *pontifex maximus* (chief priest) burst into this exclusively female space and saved the Palladium, but was blinded by the fire (or the gods) for his trouble.

The Vestals comprised a core of six formal priestesses and numerous initiates and veterans. Vestals were originally selected from Rome's greatest families when aged between six and ten, and took a solemn and strict vow of chastity and thirty years' service to Vesta. Ten years were spent learning duties and responsibilities, ten in practising them, and ten passing on skills to initiates.

Left: A marble relief in the Uffizi Collections in Florence showing the Temple of Vesta. With its links to Rome's mythological homeland of Troy and oldest traditions, it was one of the city's most important shrines.

Opposite: The Arch of the Bankers has survived almost intact, thanks to its incorporation into the church of San Giorgio in Velabro. It is covered in ornate, high relief decoration: acanthus, palmettes and egg-and-dart detailing frame subjects ranging from the sacrifice of cattle, to Hercules (the area's patron), military scenes and motifs and, most importantly, the imperial family.

Duties included tending the sacred flame, preparing sacrificial food for Rome's major cults, and officiating at state occasions.

In return, they had great privileges, such as the right to own property and make a will – uniquely for a woman in Rome's early history. They could move freely in the outside world, intervene in disputes, and were trusted guardians of aristocratic and imperial wills. They enjoyed state transport, and privileged seating at public games and festivals (the empress joined them if in attendance). With privilege came enormous responsibility. Neglecting the flame was punishable by flogging. Any Vestal who broke her vow of chastity was buried alive in a purpose-built chamber, with a small quantity of food and drink (no one should be responsible for killing a priestess), and the man involved was flogged to death. Under Domitian in the AD 80s, four Vestals were buried alive, including the *Vestalis maxima* (the chief Vestal) – and several men died with her.

In the AD 220s the emperor Elagabalus, acting for (or as!) the Syrian sun god Elagabal, not only married the chief Vestal, but also transferred the Palladium along with other sacred treasures to his new Temple of the Sun on the Palatine Hill. A century later the emperor Constantine took the Palladium to his 'new Rome' of Constantinople, a sign of old Rome's decreasing power. In AD 394 the sacred flame was extinguished forever and the Temple of Vesta was permanently closed.

The Vestals were disbanded and the last senior Vestal, Coelia Concordia, retired, but the Temple's power endured in Christian superstition and suspicion, with legends of a dragon in its cellars, fed with barley cakes (a memory of the sacred cakes baked for pagan festivals). The Temple fell in the Middle Ages, probably after an earthquake, but its remains were almost intact when rediscovered in the 1480s. Sadly, in 1540 a papal edict gave absolute licence to the Fabbrica di San Pietro, the commission for sourcing materials for the new St Peter's Basilica, and in 1549 the Temple of Vesta was all but destroyed.

Severus's **ARCH OF THE BANKERS** is in the Forum Boarium, and now partly supports the bell tower of San Giorgio in Velabro. Its inscription says it was built in AD 204 by 'ARGENTARII ET NEGOTIATORES BOARII HUIUS LOCI' (bankers and cattle merchants of this place): cattle for food and sacrifice were

a very lucrative business. Originally 7 m (23 ft) high, but now partly buried, its lower sections are undecorated travertine – practical, given passing cattle! The rest is covered in sculpted reliefs and very florid decoration, typical of the early 3rd century.

The large inner panels show the sad story of Severus's family after his death in York in northern Britain in AD 211. He told his sons to pay the troops, forget everyone else and be harmonious. Instead, Caracalla put Geta to death and the Senate decreed Geta's name should be removed from inscriptions, and all his images destroyed. This process, known to us (not to the Romans) as *damnatio memoriae* ('expunging of remembrance'), was intended to erase him from history – a clear reminder that images and inscriptions were the mass media of Roman society. This arch is perhaps one of the best examples of the phenomenon. Its large, inner panels once showed the principal members of the imperial family – Severus, his empress, Julia Domna, their children, Caracalla and Geta, Caracalla's wife Plautilla and her father Plautinus. On the right inner panel Severus and Julia Domna are sacrificing, but Geta, to the right, has gone. Opposite is Caracalla with a *patera* (sacrificial dish), but his wife and father-in-law have been chiselled away. This unsubtle 'cleansing' vividly shows how effectively the Senate's decree could erase people from the official record and, to a great extent, from public consciousness.

Opposite: A panel from the interior of the Arch shows Septimius Severus and Julia Domna making offerings at an altar. The empty right-hand side of the panel indicates where their son Geta had originally been portrayed. After his execution, all images of him and records mentioning him were destroyed – he was effectively wiped from history.

Above: One of the external panels depicts Romans with a dejected, bound captive, alluding to Severus's military prowess.

V.

AN UNCERTAIN CITY

CARACALLA

(R. AD 211–17)

ROMAN HISTORIANS PAINT Caracalla as brutal and unpopular – understandably. His murder of Geta and the subsequent purge of thousands of Geta's supporters, from senators to ordinary citizens, outraged the Senate. Luckily for Caracalla, his father's advice proved sound and the (well-) paid troops remained loyal. He fought very successful campaigns against Germanic tribes and then in the Eastern Empire (where he declared himself to be a reincarnation of Alexander the Great). Even this could not, however, ultimately save him from assassination by one of his own officers. Caracalla's biggest social achievement was granting citizenship to all free people in the Empire, but his greatest architectural legacy was the **BATHS OF CARACALLA.**

By the reign of Caracalla there were several major public baths or *thermae* in Rome, including those of Agrippa (the earliest), Nero, Titus and Trajan, and people frequented their favourites. The colossal Baths of Caracalla, or the Thermae Antoninianae (the Baths of Antoninus – Caracalla's official name), built in AD 212–16, changed the landscape of bathing and the city. At the time they were Rome's largest *thermae magnificentissimae* (most magnificent baths), literally magnifying (aggrandizing) their builder. Baths were a major resource for the people. Even more than other buildings, they were a demonstration of imperial wealth and power, because they were frequented so often and by so many.

Public baths were good propaganda, even for bad emperors. Martial wrote, 'What is worse than Nero? What is better than Nero's Baths?' Opulent *thermae* became synonymous with the good things in life. The epitaph of one Tiberius Claudius

'BATHS, WINE AND LOVE CORRUPT OUR LIVES, BUT THEY ALSO MAKE LIFE BEARABLE'

2ND CENTURY INSCRIPTION

AN UNCERTAIN CITY

The massive Baths of Caracalla, Rome's best-preserved *thermae* (public baths), accommodated over 50,000 people every week in a vast complex that included changing rooms, cold, hot and tepid rooms, saunas, exercise yards, and an enclosed garden with libraries, shops, bars, eateries and meeting rooms. The construction of the Baths and every activity within them depended on the labour of enslaved workers, the true engine of all Rome's monuments.

Secundus from the 2nd century AD says that baths, wine and love corrupt our lives, but they also make life bearable. Very importantly, cheap entry meant the baths were truly a people's palace, giving a taste of the elite's luxury to all.

Though not in the city centre, Caracalla's Baths stood near busy hubs such as the Circus Maximus and close to main roads. In fact they were set just back from the Via Appia on the specially constructed Via Nova (New Street), supposedly one of the most beautiful in Rome. The central block with the principal bathing suite was built in about AD 212–16, while the complete perimeter, with its subsidiary buildings, measuring a staggering 340 × 330 m (1,115 × 1,083 ft), was finished about twenty years later. The Baths were a mini city, with shrines, food outlets, a stadium, libraries, meeting rooms and other facilities. Around 8,000 people came here every day. Men and women were usually segregated through parallel facilities or staggered times. Mixed bathing must have happened in some establishments, though, because emperors such as Augustus and Hadrian legislated against it.

The buildings were very carefully planned. The main suite – Olympic-sized *natatio* (open-air pool), *frigidarium* (cold room),

tepidarium (warm room) and *caldarium* (hot room) – is flanked by twin sets of structures, a *palaestra* (an exercise yard – unusually, in the case of these baths, covered), changing rooms and other rooms and halls. Bathers generally progressed from the changing rooms to the *palaestra* then, in larger baths like these, to saunas and steam rooms – then the *caldarium,* the *tepidarium* and finally the *frigidarium,* before a dip in the cold *natatio.*

Each *palaestra* had two storeys, with the upper gallery paved with black and white mosaics showing such watery themes as dolphins, and cupids riding on wonderful sea beasts, including sea panthers. The ground floor was paved with multicoloured mosaics – interlocked scales or ovals and boxes, with borders of acanthus leaves. Each *palaestra* also had a great apse with mosaics showing athletes, wrestlers, boxers and umpires. Nearby were *apodyteria* or changing rooms, and stores for clothes, paved with black and white mosaics, still preserved today.

The *natatio* was a real focus, its soaring north wall resembling a theatre stage, with bronze and marble sculptures, framed by columns. Such ostentatious display conveyed a sense of luxury – and the emperor's power. Next door was the immense *frigidarium* with eight colossal Egyptian granite columns supporting its vaulted ceiling – the largest in the Roman world.

The great, round *caldarium*, its dome almost as big as the Pantheon's, was so technologically remarkable that by the 5th century AD replicating it was beyond contemporary artisans. Its heating was boosted through solar power, since much of its

Previous pages: A reconstruction of the great open-air pool (*natatio*). On the north side (right) was a massive façade, resembling a great theatre stage. It was divided up by columns of granite and marble, crusted with expensive marbles from all over the Empire and completely filled with statues. The effect of the sun on the water, the reflections on (and of) columns and sculpture would have been extraordinary.

Opposite: Caracalla's Baths
were laid out symmetrically
and each half had a great
palaestra or exercise yard.
Large balconies ran around
them at first-floor level for
viewing the activities below.
These balconies were paved
with mosaics showing marine
themes, in particular cupid
'charioteers' riding a variety
of fantastical sea creatures
including a sea panther (right).

Right: The floors of the
palaestrae were entirely
of mosaic. The great apses
contained detailed portraits
of boxers, wrestlers and
umpires, while the main area
had multicoloured geometric
patterns. Today the remaining
mosaics are damaged and
worn, but originally they were
polished to a glass-like sheen.

convex wall was a metal framework for large panes of glass. Glass mosaics covered non-glazed areas, creating a dazzling effect.

To the rear of the complex was a great porticoed *xystus*, effectively a park with trees, beds filled with flowers and shrubs, sculpture and fountains – the song of birds and cicadas mixing with the sound of running water and visitors' chatter. The soundtrack was not all pleasing, however. The writer Seneca, who lived near other baths in the city, complained about the groans of people exercising, the sound of ball games and people diving (or belly flopping) into the pools, the shouts of food- and drink-sellers, and even the cries of the body-hair remover (and the shrieks of his customers).

At the back of the park was a mini stadium, built over a huge water tank. The Baths' cisterns could hold 8 million litres (1,759,752 gallons) of water, supplied by a designated branch of the Aqua Marcia aqueduct, but curiously there is no conclusive evidence for public toilets. Bathers could at least have a good read, in one of the two-storey libraries sited at either end of the stadium.

Caracalla wanted his Baths to be Rome's largest and most glorious, to celebrate his name forever. The decoration was sumptuous, with white and coloured marbles (yellow, red, green) from Italy, North Africa, Turkey and Greece, and red and (rarer) grey granite from Egypt. Basins, pools and fountains abounded and ceilings were covered in painted stucco and glass mosaics, creating endless interactions between marble, mosaic, light and water. Every inch was covered with marble, painted plaster or glass mosaics. Brick was never visible.

CONSTRUCTING THE BATHS

THE RUINS OF the Baths of Caracalla, still towering up to 60 m (197 ft) high, are the best preserved in Rome, allowing scholars, in particular Janet DeLaine, to investigate how they were built – from materials to timescale. The statistics are incredible. The Baths swallowed up over 200,000 cubic m (7,062,933 cubic ft) of concrete, 6 million bricks, 6,500 cubic m (229,545 cubic ft) of marble and granite, 250 columns, 100 million cubes of stone for floor mosaics, and 250 million glass *tesserae* for mosaics on walls, vaults and ceilings. Just transporting materials required the equivalent of one and a half million days of ox-cart use.

Surviving fragments of sculptures and early drawings of the ruins give valuable clues about their appearance. The main Baths had over 120 statues in niches, and many others free standing. They showed Venus and Bacchus, gods of pleasure; Asclepius, god of health; athletes; and many other subjects, from emperors to heroes. Some were decorative, others were fountains, while larger sculptures acted as markers and signposts. Some imagery was pure propaganda. In both *palaestrae*, friezes showed defeated barbarians, perhaps from Caracalla's wars in Germany and Britain, more expected in a triumphalist forum. But these Baths were a kind of forum, affordable and accessible to all – a great opportunity to display imperial propaganda even while people relaxed and bathed.

An uncomfortable reality is that the Baths, in common with so much of Roman society, ran on the labour of hundreds of enslaved people. Underground, in cramped and unhealthy conditions, they maintained the water flow, delivered fuel and fed the boilers, cooked and washed; above, they looked after clothes, served food and drink, tended the gardens, cleaned, and performed many other tasks. In changing rooms, cloakroom attendants (*capsararii*) guarded clothing and possessions (rich bathers brought their own slaves). Theft was common – there was even a name for bath thieves, *fures balnearii* – though penalties were severe, including forced labour.

Under the Baths, 3 km (nearly 2 miles) of passages and tunnels were used to move all sorts of commodities, and especially wood for heating. The Baths' fifty great ovens

The ruins of the great *frigidarium* (cold room) of the Baths of Caracalla. It linked the *natatio* (pool) to the *caldarium* (hot room) and the east and the west wings. This gigantic space with its marble-lined plunge pools was a basilica, a cathedral of water, with arches and windows opening on to all surrounding spaces. Eight colossal Egyptian granite columns supported its cross-vaulted ceiling – the largest in the Roman world.

SHELLEY'S *PROMETHEUS UNBOUND* WAS WRITTEN IN THE RUINS OF THE BATHS, 'AMONG THE FLOWERY GLADES AND ODORIFEROUS BLOSSOMING TREES'

A marble sculpture of the AD 220s, known as the Farnese Hercules. This colossal statue shows the muscled demigod, exhausted after retrieving the golden apples of Hesperides. It was carved by an Athenian sculptor called Glykon, who signed the base, after a Greek bronze original of 320 BC. The statue was discovered in the Baths during excavations by the Farnese family.

consumed around 10 tons of wood every day, and a form of roundabout kept the huge daily number of wood-carts flowing. Also underground was the Mithraeum, a temple of the Persian god Mithras, the largest in Rome. Mithras, along with other monotheist deities such as Sol and the Christian God, became very popular in the 3rd and 4th centuries AD.

The Baths needed constant maintenance, and major repairs were made by Constantine in the AD 320s and King Theoderic in the 500s, but then came only decline. Not all of the heated rooms or pools were maintained, suggesting problems in sourcing fuel and water, and use effectively ceased during the Gothic Wars of the AD 530s when aqueducts were cut and the population plummeted. A major earthquake in 847 caused massive damage, and the structures deteriorated rapidly.

Farms sprang up inside the walls, and a nearby church used the area for burials. The Baths became a quarry. Even the bricks were taken away, reducing many walls to a concrete core. Marble veneer was levered off to decorate palaces and churches, or, along with many sculptures, was reduced to lime powder for mortar (or fine stucco plaster). Reused marble (*spolia*) travelled extensively and one massive granite column was taken to Florence by the Medici family. It took over a year to transport it, highlighting the immense skill of the Roman builders. Even window glass and glass *tesserae* (mosaic cubes) were recycled. Blue *tesserae*, in particular, were widely reused, including for making stained glass windows for Europe's Gothic cathedrals.

Even after centuries of pillaging, some decoration still remained *in situ* – until the excavations by Pope Paul III (Farnese) in the 1540s, who excavated and removed dozens of sculptures including the famous Farnese Hercules. The Farnese collection was taken by the family to Naples in 1788 and is now in Naples Archaeological Museum.

The Baths became an impossibly romantic ruin, covered in greenery. Shelley said his poem *Prometheus Unbound* 'was chiefly written upon the mountainous ruins of the Baths of Caracalla, among the flowery glades and odoriferous, blossoming trees'. This was all stripped away in the later 19th century.

The Baths no longer provide bathing facilities, but they still host entertainments. Since the 1930s open-air operatic performances have taken place there. Seeing an opera on a summer's evening, with Caracalla's magnificent Baths illuminated behind, is one of Rome's great experiences – an unexpected legacy of the emperor.

THE 3RD CENTURY

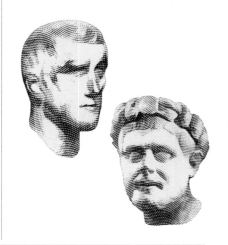

I T IS DIFFICULT to imagine the sheer scale and awfulness of the events that engulfed the Roman Empire from the AD 230s to 280s. This period of crisis, largely precipitated by imperial assassinations (starting with Geta), witnessed unprecedented and prolonged military, political and economic instability. Rival emperors clashed, cities declined or were sacked, treasuries were drained, and inflation rocketed as emperors debased the coinage to pay their troops. Without strong emperors, the Empire fell apart. In the AD 250s, Britain, France and Spain broke away, forming the Gallic Empire. Other enemies exploited Rome's weakness and poured across the Rhine and Danube frontiers, burning cities from Tarragona in Spain to Athens in Greece. They invaded Italy and even threatened Rome. Later, in the AD 260s, Queen Zenobia of Palmyra in Syria rebelled and conquered Egypt, Syria and Turkey. Add to this famine, plague and natural disasters, and the 3rd century can be seen as truly the low point of Empire.

Yet as the 3rd century lurched into its final decades there were some short-lived moments of hope. A brief respite came when Aurelian (r. AD 270–75) took the throne. Born in northwest Serbia, he was one of a number of soldier emperors from the central Balkans in this period. Aurelian was a senior cavalry commander who fought to reunite the Empire – and succeeded. He first defeated Zenobia and then accepted the surrender of the Gallic Empire, gaining the title *restitutor orbis* (Restorer of the World). In Rome, he built a massive temple to Sol Invictus (the Unconquered Sun), continuing the movement towards monotheism first championed imperially by Elagabalus fifty years earlier. The temple is completely gone, but still very

AMID THE
AWFULNESS
THAT
ENGULFED
THE ROMAN
EMPIRE
IN THE THIRD
CENTURY,
A BRIEF RESPITE
CAME WITH
AURELIAN

A reconstruction of the interior of the Aurelianic Walls, which still surround much of Rome. Made of brick and concrete, the walls stretched for 19 km (12 miles) encompassing the great expanse that the city covered by that time – a metropolis of well over a million people. The walls were punctuated by 380 towers, as well as arched passageways that facilitated the rapid movement of defenders across the circuit.

much standing is Aurelian's greatest legacy: Rome's great defensive circuit, the **AURELIANIC WALLS**.

In AD 271 barbarians came within three days of Rome. Aurelian defeated them and set about building his city walls. Completed in AD 275, they were over 19 km (12 miles) long and enclosed around 1,400 hectares (5½ square miles), encompassing Rome's seven hills and areas such as the Campus Martius and Trans Tiberim (Trastevere) on the west bank.

Unlike Rome's earlier 'Servian' tufa walls, Aurelian's were of brick-faced concrete, around 3.5 m (11½ ft) thick and 8 m (26 ft) high, with 380 tall, squared towers, set every 100 Roman feet (about 31 m, or 102 ft). Speed was clearly of the essence, and to save time and materials, some existing monuments were incorporated directly into the walls, including stretches of aqueduct and the Pyramid of Gaius Cestius. Practically, the walls protected Rome, more perhaps through deterrence than properly

functioning defence, but they also showed the emperor's willingness and ability to safeguard city and people.

In AD 311 the emperor Maxentius virtually doubled the height of the walls and strengthened the gates against his rival Constantine, but all for naught. Maxentius died in the battle of the Milvian Bridge in AD 312 and Constantine entered Rome unopposed. In the AD 400s the emperor Honorius's general, Stilicho, added the Mausoleum of Hadrian as a major bastion, increased the wall height to around 18 m (59 ft), and rounded the gate towers, embracing new defensive technology and recognizing that walls needed to work harder as manpower dwindled. These renewed defences, too, were not tested in war, and in major sackings of the city by Goths (AD 410) and Vandals (AD 455) Rome's enemies entered through treacherously opened gates.

The walls were finally tested, on a major scale, during the ruinous Gothic Wars of the AD 530–50s, with Rome endlessly taken and retaken by the Ostrogothic rulers of Italy and the Byzantines. After this, the wall circuit became increasingly disproportionate for Rome's shrunken urban area and massively

The walls were constructed hurriedly in the AD 270s after Germanic incursions into Italy. With Aurelian's troops away fighting, construction fell to Rome's guilds of masons, hence the uneven build, and the rushed, wholesale incorporation of monuments such as aqueducts and tombs. Incredibly, they were last used defensively by the Pope in 1870, against the armies of united Italy.

THE WALLS STOOD THROUGH THE CENTURIES AS A REMINDER OF ROME'S PAST AND PRESENT GLORIES

reduced population (by AD 600, perhaps around 30,000 people, compared to over a million at the time of Constantine), but stood through the centuries as a reminder of Rome's past and present glories. The walls were last defended on 20 September 1870 by Pope Pius IX's army against the forces of the newly united Italy, who wanted Rome as their capital. The siege lasted for only four hours until the wall was breached at Porta Pia in the northeast of the city. After 1,600 years, the walls stood down.

After the assassination of Aurelian in AD 275 came further chaos, with six more short-lived emperors in ten years including, in AD 283, Carinus, during whose reign a major fire devastated the Forum and the Campus Martius. Respite came in AD 285 with the accession of another Balkan military commander, Diocletian (r. AD 285–305). He appointed, effectively adopted, a trusted general, Maximian, as co-emperor – recognition that one ruler could no longer serve all the Empire's needs. The two emperors campaigned simultaneously against Rome's enemies, Maximian in the west and Diocletian in the east, reunifying the Empire and firming up its frontiers. Diocletian carried out important reforms of the civil service and the governance of Rome's provinces; he also reformed the coinage and set maximum prices for food and other commodities. Less positively, Diocletian also launched perhaps the largest ever persecution of the Christians. Thousands were martyred for the increasingly widespread religion.

The two emperors ruled harmoniously, and in an unprecedented move, in AD 305, they abdicated voluntarily, in favour of their successors – four in total, a senior ruler (Augustus) and a deputy (Caesar) in both East and West. This 'Tetrarchy', from the Greek 'rule of four', could have worked, had their successors possessed the same collegiality. Sadly for the Empire, they didn't.

In Rome, Diocletian and Maximian set about rebuilding and restoring monuments including Caesar's Forum, the Curia and the Temple of Saturn. In their own right they dedicated in AD 306 the immense **BATHS OF DIOCLETIAN**, the largest in the Empire, eclipsing even the great Baths of Caracalla built a century before. Caracalla's Baths preserve the atmosphere, the layout and the scale of the ancient baths, but Diocletian's are interesting more for their varied reuse and long-enduring impact on their surroundings.

Although more integrated into the fabric of, and more damaged by, the modern city, they are still impressive. The precinct occupied a colossal area of about 380 × 370 m (around 12 hectares,

or almost 30 acres) with the Baths themselves covering a huge 250 × 180 m (820 × 590½ ft). The curve of today's Piazza della Repubblica follows the line of the great semi-circular enclosure (*exedra*) at the rear of the complex, hence the square's other name, 'Piazza dell'Esedra'. The Baths of Diocletian, like other great imperial *thermae*, had an axial plan of hot, cold, tepid rooms and pool, flanked by sets of buildings including *palaestrae* (exercise yards). They also offered, on a very grand scale, clubrooms, gymnasia, gardens, shops and libraries – including the famous Bibliotheca Ulpia, transferred from Trajan's Forum.

The Baths ceased to function after the cutting of Rome's aqueducts in the Gothic Wars of the mid-6th century. They were now unserviceable in terms of water and fuel and, not least, customers and staff, with the collapse of Rome's population to perhaps just 5 per cent of what it had been under Diocletian. Even had there been public demand, the Church viewed mass bathing (as opposed to baptism) as a worldly pleasure and highly undesirable.

In the late 11th century, a church was established on the site (after a ceremony of purification to banish any lingering pagan

The Baths of Diocletian from above. They have been altered and damaged over the centuries, used as everything from a grain store to a jail and even a planetarium, but much of the original plan survives. Many spaces still have their roofs, such as the cold room (*frigidarium*), centre left, now Santa Maria degli Angeli (St Mary of the Angels).

AN UNCERTAIN CITY

A 16th-century reconstruction of the Baths of Diocletian. The Baths were a favourite subject for Renaissance artists and draughtsmen, who recorded much of the structures and decoration as being well preserved. This changed in the following 200 years, thanks to the increasingly desperate hunt for building materials. As recently as the later 19th century, the remains of the massive *exedra* (apse), at the bottom of the picture, made way for the major Via Nazionale.

spirits), but otherwise the ruins lay sufficiently outside the built-up area of the city, and so the structures remained largely intact until the Renaissance. A visitor in 1450 recorded many columns and other decorative features still *in situ*, and the numerous drawings of the ruins show many rooms still with their vaulted roofs – some survive today. One of these, to the left of the church of Santa Maria degli Angeli (St Mary of the Angels) is the Sala Ottagona, a well-preserved octagonal hall which in recent history served as the city's planetarium and is now used for exhibitions. The domed ceiling has a Pantheon-style *oculus* (central opening) – here, appropriately, octagonal – lessening the stress on the dome and letting in light.

From the Renaissance the area became busier, with houses, villas, parks and new roads. Many rooms in the Baths became papal storehouses for grain and oil, as essential for the popes to control and distribute as they had been for the emperors. A Certosa or monastery was inserted into the Baths in the 1560s, with two courtyards, the larger probably the work of Michelangelo who, in 1564, also transformed the great *frigidarium* (cold room) into the church of Santa Maria degli Angeli. The vaulting, 33 m (108 ft) high, and most of the red granite columns are original, but a quick knock on others reveals they are painted plaster.

Unlike the building of the Certosa, later interventions caused major damage to the Baths. In the 1580s Pope Sixtus V

Previous pages: A reconstruction of the bustling, beautifully appointed *frigidarium* (cold room) of the Baths of Diocletian. Every inch is covered with marble, gilded stucco and mosaic, and a host of statues crowd the space. No expense was spared in these Baths – the largest in the Roman world and a sign of Diocletian's power and munificence.

Opposite: A very different view of the *frigidarium* today, as the church of Santa Maria degli Angeli, converted by Michelangelo in the 1560s. The original Roman decoration has all gone but the coloured marbles still evoke some of the building's splendour. The immense proportions and soaring columns are also preserved (even if some of the columns are plaster copies).

demolished about a fifth of the total remaining structures – including the massive, round *caldarium* (hot room) – sometimes using gunpowder. As late as the 1870s a major road, the Via Nazionale, cut through the *exedra* at the rear, which disappeared completely soon afterwards.

Following Rome's establishment as capital in 1871 the area became fully urbanized. The new Termini railway station was built and residential areas swept away many of the great houses and parks which had characterized the location. The monastery closed in the 1880s, and much of the Baths became the National Archaeological Museum delle Terme (of the Baths), though other parts were used for an orphanage, a poorhouse and a prison. Even into the 20th century, up until the final occupation by the Museum of all the Baths in 1911, the Museum shared the site with a hotel, a hospice for the blind and the Caffe Concerto Diocleziano. The Museum still occupies the site, though its collections are jointly displayed with the nearby Palazzo Massimo.

The Baths had an enormous impact during their lifetime. They were the largest such complex, reshaping this whole area of Rome. But they also had a varied and unexpected impact in their afterlife, as everything from church to café and oil store to planetarium – a legacy far greater than Diocletian and Maximian could have imagined.

Sadly, their intended great legacy, the Tetrarchy, with its multiple rulers serving the Empire together, collapsed very quickly after their retirement AD 305, and once again rival rulers fought for imperial power.

MAXENTIUS

(R. AD 306–12)

THE LAST OF the pagan emperors to conduct a major building programme of secular and pagan monuments in Rome was Maxentius, son of Diocletian's co-emperor Maximian. Having ousted Galerius (Diocletian's appointee) and declared himself emperor, he restored the Temple of Venus and Roma and built the Temple of Divus Romulus and the immense Basilica of Maxentius nearby. Meanwhile, far away in Britain, his rival Constantine, now declared Augustus by his legions, started to plan his next moves.

Maxentius, like his father, wanted to restore the status and glory of his capital of Rome – undermined by the many-centred Tetrarchy and devastated by the fire of Carinus in AD 283. He strengthened the city walls, restored the great Temple of Venus and Roma, using the polychrome columns and marbles so favoured in the early 4th century AD, and in AD 306 he constructed the **BASILICA OF MAXENTIUS** (Basilica Nova), later the Basilica of Constantine. Its site had once been occupied by warehouses – the Horrea Piperataria – which stored *piper* (pepper) but also other spices and herbs, including medicinal ones. This was handy for the city's medical community, located nearby, including the famous gladiators' doctor Galen. The fire of AD 283 left this once-packed quarter a gutted ruin – a perfect opportunity for Maxentius to build.

Today, even as a ruin, the Basilica of Maxentius dominates this area, but complete it was stunning and architecturally revolutionary. The Basilica was the last structure to be built in the Forum Romanum and, at over 80 m (262 ft) long, was the largest single vaulted space in the Roman Empire. It was modelled not on the aisled basilicas such as the Basilica Julia,

MAXENTIUS WANTED TO RESTORE THE STATUS AND GLORY OF ROME

Below: A view of the eastern end of the Forum Romanum, looking towards the three remaining arches of the Basilica of Maxentius. The largest of Rome's basilicas, it was a symbol of Maxentius's commitment to Rome.

Overleaf: A reconstruction of the towering interior of the Basilica. It was the largest vaulted space in the Empire, modelled not on the traditional aisled basilicas but on the soaring halls of the great baths.

but on the great vaulted halls of the Baths of Diocletian (dedicated in the same year). But Maxentius's Basilica was even bigger and grander. The remaining arches, 25 m (82 ft) high, formed just one aisle, with a parallel aisle flanking the great vaulted nave, which soared to a height of 35 m (115 ft), and was decorated with coffering in hexagons and lozenges, all stuccoed, painted and gilded. This multicoloured coffering created an incredible spectacle overhead, but also, as in the Pantheon, served to lighten the mass of the concrete ceiling. It inspired the architecture of many later buildings, in particular the coffered ceilings of the aisles of St Peter's.

Buildings, of course, spoke of an emperor's wealth and power (and benevolence) but even the construction process could impress, vividly displaying the resources at his command. Monolithic Corinthian columns of white Proconnesian marble from Turkey, 15 m (49 ft) high, and weighing more than 90 tons, supported each of the eight springs of the Basilica's coffered nave ceiling. Just getting these to Rome was an amazing feat but to move them through the city required around twenty-five pairs of oxen – an enormous cattle train – giving onlookers a vivid reminder of their city's glory and their emperor's power.

The Basilica's interior was a paradise. The floor and walls were completely covered in multicoloured marble, peppered with statue-filled niches. The great windows were filled with geometric traceries of glass, while above, the sky-like ceiling glittered like a great canopy. At the west end, in a great apse, was a colossal seated statue of Maxentius, originally 15 m (49 ft) high. If made of solid stone it would have gone through the floor, so the limbs and head were marble, with the body made of wood, covered in gilded bronze. After the death of Maxentius in AD 312, Constantine replaced the statue's head

Opposite: Huge coffered arches made up the Basilica's gigantic side aisles. As in the Pantheon, coffering allowed the structure to be strong without too much weight. Each concentric octagonal panel was filled with gilded and brightly coloured stucco. The walls were covered in marble, their niches filled with sculptures of deities and emperors.

Right: In the great western apse was a colossal seated sculpture of Maxentius, with marble head and limbs and a wooden framework body, covered in gilded sheet bronze. After Maxentius's death, Constantine claimed the monument and put his own likeness on the statue. These elements of the statue, including the head, were discovered in the apse in 1486.

with his own likeness. He also modified the building, adding a large north apse and another entrance directly onto the Via Sacra and Forum.

After Empire the Basilica's importance dwindled, especially because it was never converted into a church. In AD 629 its gilded bronze tiles were removed for St Peter's, and in AD 847 an earthquake brought down one aisle and part of the nave, the rest probably falling in the great earthquake of 1349. The Basilica became merely a quarry, and in 1457, stone robbers in the western apse found the head and limbs of the colossal statue of Constantine/Maxentius (now in the Capitoline Museums). The Basilica's marble pavement of coloured circles and squares was very well preserved when uncovered in the Renaissance, but sadly the use of the ruins as a barn, riding school and finally, in the 1840s, as a military drill hall destroyed the floor completely. One of the Basilica's great columns was still *in situ* in the 1600s when it was taken away to be the pedestal for the statue of the Virgin Mary in front of Santa Maria Maggiore.

With his Basilica, Maxentius transformed part of the Forum Romanum into (he hoped) an eternal glorification of himself and his line. His legacy was short-lived, however, thanks to Constantine.

VI.

FROM
OLD
TO NEW

CONSTANTINE

(R. AD 306–37)

CONSTANTINE WAS ARGUABLY the greatest beneficiary of the Tetrarchy system. He was not one of those originally appointed as Augustus or Caesar, but he was the son of one of the Caesars, Constantius, and he had ambition. Starting from his legionary power base in Britain in AD 310, in just over a decade, through supreme military ability, ruthlessness and some good luck, he became sole ruler of the Empire. He reformed the currency, the army and the civil service, leaving systems that would last effectively for the rest of the empire.

He is often considered – incorrectly – to be Rome's first Christian emperor. Rather, he was the first emperor to tolerate Christianity officially, proceeding to give it preferential treatment, personally intervening in major church decisions, and finally making it, in effect, the state religion. He also founded a new, Christian capital at Byzantium (Istanbul), renaming it – after himself – Constantinople. Crucially, this removed the seat of the emperor from Rome for good. This exacerbated the existing East/West split of the Empire and was to have profound and negative consequences for the city of Rome.

Constantine's focus was on Constantinople, but no emperor could yet afford to be seen to neglect Rome. To enhance the city (and to be seen doing so), he built the last great arch, the Arch of Constantine, the last imperial baths (though small compared to those of Caracalla or Diocletian) and put his name to Maxentius's Basilica. Most importantly, however, Constantine's building programme produced the first imperial churches – including St Peter's, San Giovanni in Laterano (St John Lateran), and St Paul Outside the Walls.

CONSTANTINE'S FOCUS WAS ON CONSTANTINOPLE, BUT NO EMPEROR COULD BE SEEN TO NEGLECT ROME

The Arch of Constantine, Rome's last and best preserved triumphal arch, commemorated his defeat of Maxentius in AD 312. Sited near the Colosseum and the entrance to the Forum Romanum, it firmly asserted Constantine's authority. Most of the decoration covering the Arch was not contemporary to Constantine but dates to earlier emperors such as Trajan and Hadrian.

In a very prominent position, near the Colosseum and the entrance to the Forum Romanum, stood the **ARCH OF CONSTANTINE**, 25 m (82 ft) high, 26 m (85 ft) wide, and the last great secular monument of ancient Rome. It was dedicated to Constantine in AD 315 by the Senate, to commemorate his victory over Maxentius on 28 October AD 312. Extensive use of multi-period *spolia* could suggest decreasing availability of new materials and the resulting cannibalization of older (pagan) monuments, and perhaps the decreasing availability (or ability) of artists and artisans. One interesting, though controversial, idea is that Constantine did not build the Arch at all, but simply refaced an arch built earlier, perhaps by Hadrian. Either way, it is the most complex of Rome's surviving arches. At the top of both north (Colosseum) and south sides are inscriptions, in which the emperor acknowledges that he owes his victory over Maxentius to the '... *INSTINCTU DIVINITATIS* ...' (inspiration of a/the God) and also, in true imperial style, records '...*MENTIS MAGNITUDINE*...' (the greatness of [Constantine's] mind). This 'inspiration' was, perhaps, Constantine's supposed vision of Christ's Cross before the battle of the Milvian Bridge.

Flanking the inscriptions are Dacian (Romanian) prisoners, with trousers, straggly beards and moustaches. These carvings date to around AD 100, in the reign of Trajan, while the large rectangular sculptures date to Marcus Aurelius in the AD 160s. Facing south are scenes from the emperor's German wars, showing him overseeing captured chieftains, or officiating at a *suovetaurilia* sacrifice (a very solemn sacrifice of a sheep, pig and an ox) with military standards behind. North shows his triumphal return to Rome, sitting in the Forum, with suitably cowed barbarians, and garlanded columns of public buildings behind. Everywhere the head of Marcus Aurelius has been modified to resemble Constantine, a simple but effective rebranding.

Also striking is the use of coloured stone. Some columns were light yellow, while the roundels, taken from a monument of Hadrian of the AD 130s, were all originally reset against purple porphyry. On the south the emperor hunts and sacrifices to Diana, goddess of the hunt. On the north he sacrifices again, this time to Apollo, Diana's brother, and is then shown standing over a dead lion. This may commemorate the lion hunt in the desert, which took place during Hadrian's visit to Egypt with his court and his male lover Antinous in AD 130.

Amid all the *spolia* are some Constantinian elements. The roundels on the short sides show Luna, goddess of the moon, in her elegant two-horse chariot (*biga*) and Sol, god of the sun, in his four-horse racer (*quadriga*). Winged Victories flank the main arch, but their wings and hairstyles are heavier and less

Opposite, above: At the top of both sides of the Arch is a lengthy inscription, telling how Constantine vanquished the 'tyrant', i.e. Maxentius, flanked by statues of prisoners. These are not followers of Maxentius, but Romanian warriors, captured by Trajan two hundred years earlier – an example of the Arch's 'recycling'.

Opposite, below: On the short ends of the Arch are roundels of Constantinian date, showing the Moon and, here, the Sun. Constantine favoured Christianity, but he knew he was dealing with a predominantly pagan city and his imagery remained deliberately ambivalent.

Right: A detail from the north side of the Arch includes two roundels from a monument of Hadrian built in the AD 130s, while the relief below shows Constantine distributing largesse to the people two centuries later.

lively than those on the Arch of Septimus Severus in the Forum Romanum, carved only a century before, reflecting the changed artistic landscape and reduced resources after the difficult 3rd century. The abundant, deliberate reuse of overtly pagan scenes is striking, reflecting the continued strength of paganism in Rome and the potential ambivalence of the religious beliefs of many, including Constantine himself.

The contemporary narrow frieze that wraps around the Arch shows events leading up to Constantine's final victory over Maxentius. Constantine sets out with his army from Milan, his troops wearing late Roman clothing, such as leggings and pill-box hats, then storms Verona (with Victory overhead) and, arriving at the gates of Rome, fights Maxentius. The battle is ferocious and chaotic, and the River Tiber churns with bodies. Finally Constantine enters Rome in triumph on a chariot, and is then shown in the Forum, enthroned on the Rostra, with the Arch of Septimius Severus on the right and the Basilica Julia on the left. He distributes money to the people – one man even lifts his child up to get a better view. The column bases show soldiers taking away Maxentius's followers as prisoners, while Victory records Constantine's success on ceremonial shields.

The important position of the Arch and its link with the 'Christian' emperor Constantine ensured its survival. Prominent in the artistic consciousness of Rome, it appears in Italian Renaissance art, for example in the background of scenes painted by Botticelli and Perugino in the Sistine Chapel. In a fascinating postscript, excavations near the Arch in 2006 found a cache of

items including ceremonial lances and sceptres – perhaps
the personal regalia of Maxentius, buried (ironically enough)
in the shadow of his rival's monument.

Set in the southeast of the city, just inside the walls,
is Rome's cathedral church, the Basilica of **SAN GIOVANNI IN
LATERANO**. The church is named 'in Laterano' because it was
built on the site of the palace and estate of the wealthy Roman
Laterani family. It has few (visible) ancient remains, except
for a collection of inscriptions and architecture in the cloister
and its great bronze doors, dating to the 2nd century AD, brought
here from the Senate House in the 1660s. But archaeology
under and around the Basilica has revealed numerous buildings
including a palatial villa. Probably awarded by the emperor
Septimius Severus to the general Titus Sextus Lateranus around
AD 200, the villa was vast and richly decorated, with some walls
marble-veneered to a height of over 6 m (20 ft).

Opposite: The Basilica of San Giovanni in Laterano (St John Lateran). Constantine built several churches at Rome, but given the city's paganism, only a few were within the walls. Imperial attention and funding turned increasingly to Christianity, good news for churches but not for Rome's other monuments.

Right: The Baptistery of San Giovanni, or the church of San Giovanni in Fonte (Saint John of the Spring) was built in about AD 430 behind the Basilica, and is the oldest surviving baptistery in the Empire. Celebrants were baptized in opulent surroundings, with porphyry and marble columns and veneer, polychrome mosaics and statues of bronze and silver. The new religion gave its followers all the beauty and trappings of the old.

In the AD 190s, Septimius Severus had added to this part of Rome the *castra nova*, the 'new fort' of imperial horse guards (*equites singulares*). This joined the imperial 'Sessorian' palace (complete with its own private arena and circus), and a group of existing forts, in the east and southeast of the city, essentially militarizing and imperializing it. One of these other forts, with barracks buildings and a fine house, perhaps for the commander, was found in 2016 during construction of a new Metro line and will be incorporated into the Porta Metronia station. Septimius's 'new fort' was set on a massive brick and concrete platform, completely reshaping the area, and was strongly defended, its wall reinforced with numerous squared towers. It was filled with dense, neat rows of barracks, around a *principia* (headquarters building) finely decorated with mosaics, frescoes and statues. This fort manifested Septimius Severus's power and authority, reminding the people that their emperor was truly *imperator*

(supreme commander of the armed forces), and could use those forces when, and against whom, he wished. In AD 312 Constantine razed the fort, a punishment for the horse guards' support for Maxentius. He confiscated the site and on it he built his huge Christian basilica. It was centred on the *principia*, though, at around 100 m (328 ft) long, it was much larger. Dedicated first to Christ the Saviour and later, to St John the Evangelist and St John the Baptist, it was intended to be the seat of the Bishop of Rome – the home of the papal chair or *cathedra* – and so the first cathedral in Rome (and the Empire). Archaeologists have reconstructed its plan and interior, with five great aisles, its major nave colonnades made of massive, reused red granite columns. There was also an ornate *fastigium* (altar screen), supported by bronze Corinthian columns and decorated with large silver statues of Christ, the disciples and angels. The columns, now in the north transept of the cathedral, were supposedly brought from the Temple of Jupiter Optimus Maximus – from the home of the old god to the home of the new.

In terms of Rome's buildings, Constantine was focused firmly on churches, both constructing them and giving them generous endowments and gifts. This underlined and encouraged a major shift in Roman society. Imperial resources had changed direction, increasingly away from buildings serving the general public good, and towards churches serving God, the growing Christian community and the will of their emperor (and later the popes). Any aristocrats who needed or wanted imperial approval or support followed suit. Later Roman wealth was finite, and growing support for Christian buildings necessarily had a negative impact on older secular or pagan monuments.

Behind San Giovanni stands an octagonal baptistery, correctly known as San Giovanni in Fonte (St John of the Font). The Roman world's oldest surviving (legal) baptistery, it was built in the AD 430s, probably on the site of an earlier baptistery erected by Constantine. Massive porphyry columns flank the entrance leading into the font area, surrounded by two octagonal tiers of columns in deep red porphyry and white marble. Celebrants stood in the font while holy water (originally from the Aqua Claudia aqueduct) was poured over them. According to legend – and the inscription on the nearby obelisk – Constantine himself was baptized here, but this more probably happened on his deathbed, in Nicomedia near Constantinople.

The baptistery was filled with mosaics, expensive marble veneer and statues in precious metal. Sadly, much of the decoration was destroyed in later rebuilding, while the statues were stolen

OBELISKS EVOKED THE ANCIENT AUTHORITY AND WEALTH OF EGYPT, AND THEIR REMOVAL TO ROME SYMBOLIZED THE HANDING OVER OF THAT LEGACY

The San Giovanni Obelisk, at 32 m (105 ft) by far the tallest in Rome, was discovered in pieces in the Circus Maximus and was re-erected here by the Pope in 1587. Like a Roman emperor, the Pope wanted to show his munificence and harness the monument's power – both Egyptian and imperial Roman.

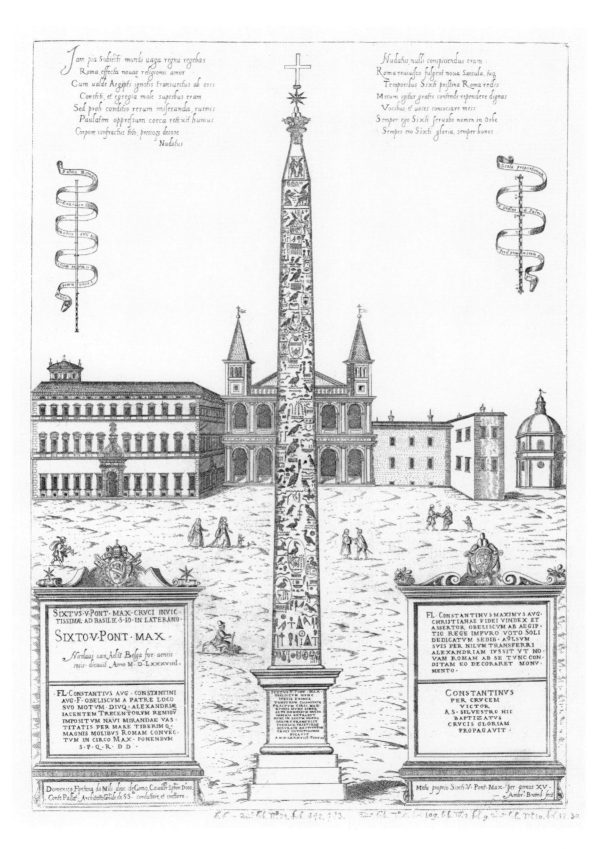

Today the Obelisk has lost its political meaning but is still one of the most impressive freestanding monuments in the city. The hieroglyphs, now readable, say it was originally set up around 1400 BC in Thebes, Egypt. Latin inscriptions tell how Constantine tried and failed to transport the Obelisk to 'New Rome' (Constantinople). In AD 357, one of his sons, Constantius II, finally brought it to 'old' Rome and set it up in the Circus Maximus.

during Rome's several sacks. The Vandals in AD 455 were not choosy about whose gold and silver they pillaged. Along with Christian church plate and statuary, and the gilded tiles from the Temple of Capitoline Jupiter, they took the Great Menorah looted by Vespasian from the Temple of Jerusalem, placed in the Temple of Peace, and reputedly given to San Giovanni for safekeeping after the sack of Alaric in AD 410.

In the square in front of the baptistery is the **SAN GIOVANNI OBELISK**. There are over a dozen obelisks in Rome, but this one is special. At over 32 m (105 ft) high and weighing a mighty 300 tons it is the tallest and largest ancient obelisk still standing in Rome (and the world) and, dating to around 1400 BC, it is also the oldest. Its inscription relates how it was first set up in the Temple of Amun-Ra at Thebes by the pharaoh Thutmose III in around 1400 BC. Constantine took it from there to Alexandria ready to be shipped to Rome. But even Constantine was defeated by the logistics of transport, so it lay in Alexandria for decades. Constantius II, one of Constantine's sons, finally pulled off this technological feat with the help of a 300-oared ship 'of remarkable size'. In AD 357 he brought the Obelisk across the sea and up the River Tiber to Rome, then placed it on the central reserve (*spina*) of the Circus Maximus.

Obelisks evoked the immeasurable age of Egypt, with its authority and wealth, but their transport and setting up in Rome symbolized the handing over of that legacy. Constantius II never lived in Rome – and indeed only visited it once – but it was still expedient, even for a Constantinopolitan emperor, to honour the Eternal City. In 1587 the Obelisk was discovered where it had fallen in the Circus Maximus, and the Pope decided to re-erect it near San Giovanni. Eventually he chose the spot where, until the 1540s, the equestrian statue of Marcus Aurelius had been displayed. One symbol of power and Roman authority had replaced another.

Constantine's building programme – providing for some secular structures, but focusing on churches – set the tone for the 4th century and beyond. After his death in AD 337 his sons fought among themselves for the Empire, and differences over religion became increasingly bitter, first between pagans and Christians and then between the various sects of Christianity. In terms of building, imperial energies were focused very much on the new religion and the new capital at Constantinople.

LATE PAGANS

THERE WERE STILL pagans in Roman society, however, some of them very wealthy and devout. For a brief period (AD 361–63) there was even a pagan (certainly non-Christian) emperor, Julian, who cleverly tried to reverse the ascendancy of the new religion not by burning its adherents, but by removing their privileged tax status and other practical measures. If his reign had been longer, history might well have been different. Yet even though he restored lands and funds to the temples and tried to reinvigorate pagan priesthoods and festivals, the time for new public buildings, whether pagan or secular, had truly passed. Indeed, the emperor Valentinian in the later AD 360s said Rome had enough public buildings and effectively forbade any new structures. Fire and age, however, did give opportunities for repair and renewal. In spite of papal and imperial disapproval and legislation, pagans restored monuments, especially in the still solidly pagan Forum Romanum, including the Temple of Saturn and the Portico of the Harmonious Gods.

Towering over the southern end of the Forum is the façade of the **TEMPLE OF SATURN**. Its columns now look strange and isolated, because the temple walls have disappeared, along with the staircase providing access from the Forum.

The first Temple of Saturn, dating back to the 490s BC, was one of the earliest to be constructed in Republican Rome, and was rebuilt in 42 BC by Lucius Munatius Plancus – who threw the banquet at which Cleopatra famously dissolved a pearl in her wine. The Temple also had a secular function, housing part of the city treasury (so brazenly pillaged by Julius Caesar), traces of which are still visible in front of the podium.

DESPITE PAPAL AND IMPERIAL DISAPPROVAL, PAGAN MONUMENTS CONTINUED TO BE RESTORED

The Temple of Saturn was one of the oldest in Rome, but the remains seen today are from a restoration, probably in the AD 360–370s, when Christianity was the emperor's religion but not yet Rome's. The façade's inscription tells of a restoration by the Senate and the Roman people: a defiant message to the emperor that paganism was not finished yet.

Saturn – the Greek god Kronos, the Earth Father – was one of the oldest established deities linked to Rome, presiding over agriculture, livestock and the countryside. Myth said that, exiled from Greece by Zeus, he came to Italy and Rome where, encouraged by the double-faced Janus (another refugee), he set up a city called Saturnia on the Capitoline Hill, and presided over a 'golden age' long before the arrival of Romulus or Hercules. Inside the Temple was an ancient statue of the god, probably of wood or ivory, veiled and holding a pruning knife – emphasizing his link to agriculture. His feet, curiously, were bound with woollen ropes, which were cut on the occasion of his festival, the Saturnalia.

The Temple of Saturn, as seen now, is almost certainly a late 4th-century AD restoration. The inscription tellingly records how the Senate and the people of Rome (not the emperor, who by then was usually Christian) restored the Temple, gutted by fire, '*INCENDIO CONSUMPTUM*'. Unusually, the column capitals (matching and probably carved specially for the restoration) are in elegant, early, Ionic style, not the normal imperial Corinthian. Another striking feature is the use of clearly mismatched and reused column elements – drums of different thickness and

SATURNALIA

THE ROMAN FESTIVAL of Saturnalia ran from 17–19 December, so did not cover 25 December – the date of the winter solstice. In that sense it is not the direct ancestor of Christmas, but there were many similarities in customs and features.

Labour in the fields and business in the banks and law courts temporarily ceased, candles and lamps were lit to brighten the winter darkness and everyone could let their hair down. There may even have been a period of licence for slaves when they could drink and dine freely (perhaps dine with their masters – or even be served by them) and speak frankly – though a wise slave would always remember that Saturnalia had to end.... More general licence in the free community seems to have involved discarding the 'business attire' toga, and generally a great increase in drinking, feasting, dancing, singing and gambling.

People gave presents, especially on the last day of the festivities, Sigillaria (named after *sigilla* or clay figurines, a common gift). A list, possibly exaggerated (or maybe not!), from the poet Martial lists figurines, board games, literary works, balls, lamps, make-up, drinking cups, clothing, soft furnishings and live animals and birds, and many other gifts, with short mottoes – in effect gift tags – to accompany them. All the while the cry of 'Io Saturnalia' rang through streets and houses. Not everyone approved. The writer Pliny took himself off to a suite of rooms at his villa so he wouldn't be a damp squib for the revellers – and they wouldn't annoy him. Much to the disquiet of Rome's Christian rulers, the festival seems to have lived on long after paganism was banned.

mismatched bases. From the interior it is clear the entablature is also reused. The extensive use of *spolia* is often read as a sign of difficulty – even for senators – in finding good materials in the late Empire. Others think the use of *spolia* here was deliberate – a bringing together of Rome's past structures and glories into an archaic, senatorial (not imperial) reconstruction. Either way, this temple was a very clear example of pagan aristocrats still active in public benefaction, at a time of rapid Christianization – a statement of steadfastness and defiance (but to the Christians, a provocation).

Under the towering mass of the Tabularium (record office) was another late antique pagan monument, the **PORTICO OF THE HARMONIOUS GODS**. As with so many of Rome's monuments, the Portico was probably first built to curry divine favour during Rome's Republican period wars. It comprised six rooms flanked with columns, in which were twelve gilded statues of the major Roman gods, grouped in pairs, including spouses (Jupiter and Juno), siblings (Apollo and Diana) and lovers (Venus and Mars). It was restored in AD 367 by the senator

The unique Portico of the Harmonious Gods, just beyond the Temple of Saturn, comprised a colonnade and connected rooms containing gilded bronze statues of the twelve major pagan deities of Rome. These were 'harmoniously' displayed in natural pairs, such as Venus and her lover Mars, or Jupiter and his queen Juno. The Portico was the last pagan monument to be built in Rome.

Vettius Agorius Praetextatus. He was the *praefectus urbi* (Prefect of the City of Rome), the most senior official under the emperor, and a trusted supporter of the pagan emperor Julian. When criticized by Pope Damasus I for his stubborn paganism, Praetextatus replied that if Damasus made him the Bishop of Rome (i.e. pope), he'd convert immediately. Power and status in late antiquity were as important as ever. With the final passing of paganism, the fate of the Portico's statues, of such symbolic and intrinsic value, can be easily imagined. The Portico itself was preserved by being completely buried in debris washed down from the Capitoline Hill, until its rediscovery in the 1830s.

The impact of seeing these two overtly pagan monuments together in the Forum, so close to the Curia where a very important and symbolic battle over the pagan altar of Victory had raged for decades, would have been considerable – an inspiration to embattled pagans and an insufferable challenge, if only temporary, to the growing power of Christianity. There was no doubt of the ultimate victor in this conflict, however. Waves of legislation eroded paganism's remaining authority and its social and financial basis. The Curia altar (the embodiment of paganism and pagan sacrifice) was finally removed by Gratian

in AD 382. The pagan senator Symmachus and Bishop Ambrose of Milan both wrote impassioned letters to the emperor for and against reinstating the altar, and Ambrose prevailed – a body blow to pagan Rome. In the 380s/390s, a series of decrees by Theodosius I effectively outlawed paganism, and drove its remnants underground. First, pagan sacrifice – through incense or blood – along with any frequenting of temples and shrines was made illegal, and then in AD 393 any form of pagan worship, whether private or public, was banned. It was also Theodosius who, at his death, nominated his two sons Honorius and Arcadius to rule the East and West respectively. Following this fateful decision, the Empire would never again be reunited.

Yet, though paganism was banned, the monuments themselves, as civic assets, were often given imperial protection, as long as they were no longer associated with any perceived source of evil, i.e. pagan altars. At this time Rome's population was still around a million and the city looked and functioned as an imperial capital though, importantly, without the emperors, who now resided elsewhere, the Eastern ruler in Constantinople and the Western in the more easily defended city of Ravenna, in northeast Italy.

The Temple of Saturn (centre) and the Portico of the Harmonius Gods (left). These monuments marked a late pagan flourish, but from the time of Constantine the emperors, with very few exceptions, were Christian, and this affected Rome's monuments. Wealth and favour increasingly passed to Christianity, and only twenty-five years after the rebuilding of these last pagan monuments, paganism was outlawed.

FROM OLD TO NEW

IN THIS PERIOD THE FIRST MAJOR PUBLIC BUILDINGS START DISAPPEARING FROM THE RECORD

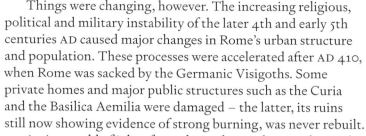

Things were changing, however. The increasing religious, political and military instability of the later 4th and early 5th centuries AD caused major changes in Rome's urban structure and population. These processes were accelerated after AD 410, when Rome was sacked by the Germanic Visigoths. Some private homes and major public structures such as the Curia and the Basilica Aemilia were damaged – the latter, its ruins still now showing evidence of strong burning, was never rebuilt.

An inexorable flight of population began, because beyond the physical damage to Rome, there was very real psychological trauma at this violation of the supposedly Eternal City. Rome was now unsafe. Already deserted by the emperor and his court and increasingly by the aristocracy and their large households (and dependents), Rome quickly began to lose its importance. To compound this, the food supplies so essential to a massive, complex city became unreliable, partly due to barbarian invasions, in particular the Vandal capture of the corn- and olive oil-rich province of Africa.

Within decades of the sack of AD 410, the number of inhabitants fell to perhaps only half a million. Huge numbers of habitations, from mansions to tenement blocks, were abandoned over large swathes of the city. People began to gravitate towards the centre, in particular the monumental area of the Campus Martius. The emperors Arcadius and Honorius had to pass laws threatening exile and confiscation of property to whoever tried to build shacks (*tuguria*) in the Campus Martius, in particular, perhaps, in the precincts of the now redundant temples. And the living were not the only problem. From the early 5th century AD burials began to appear within the city walls – something unthinkable in the Classical period (and absolutely taboo to pagans).

From the mid- to later 5th century, archaeology reveals soil accumulating in some monumental piazzas, and it is in this period that the first major public buildings (often pagan) start disappearing from the record, including Augustus's great Temple of Mars Ultor and Vespasian's Temple of Peace. Further and more serious sacks of Rome followed in AD 455 and 475 and after this the city's architectural landscape really began to change, and the population nose-dived to perhaps 200,000 or fewer. Many buildings were damaged, or succumbed to age, fire and flood. Increasingly – especially with regard to pagan or secular monuments – buildings ceased to be repaired and maintained. As a result, some monuments became quarries for materials – especially for churches.

CHRISTIANS

<DURING THE 4TH century, emperors – even the all-powerful
Constantine – had dared to build only one church, San
Giovanni in Laterano, within the walls of pagan Rome,
and then only on his own land. In the 5th century many more
followed, no longer at the margins of the city or outside the
walls but (like San Clemente and Santi Giovanni e Paolo near
the Colosseum) in much more central areas.

The grandest and best preserved of these 5th-century
churches is the great Basilica of **SANTA MARIA MAGGIORE**
(St Mary Major). In the Christian Empire, the format of the
basilica, intended for commerce, legal matters and gatherings
of the people, became a blueprint for major churches. Santa
Maria Maggiore has, of course, changed since its creation
in the early 5th century, but its form and decoration would
still be very recognizable to ancient Romans. Long aisles of
ancient, reused columns support the main body of the church.
Its coffered ceiling – though later overlaid with the first gold
brought from the Americas by Christopher Columbus – is
Roman in design, as are the vaulted ceilings in the aisles,
just as in the secular basilicas.

Dating to the Basilica's dedication in AD 432 are the mosaic
bands of acanthus scrolls running above the columns in the nave,
and the small square panels above these showing scenes from
the Old Testament. These very Classical mosaics depict in great
detail people wearing distinctively late Roman clothing,
cityscapes – and lots of sheep. In the later, more Byzantine-style
apse mosaic, Christ and Mary are shown looking like an emperor
and empress of Byzantium with huge expanses of gold, peppered
with angels. The overall impression of the decor is sumptuous

THE FORMAT OF THE CLASSICAL BASILICA BECAME A BLUEPRINT FOR MAJOR CHURCHES

The Basilica of Santa Maria Maggiore (St Mary Major) was one of many churches built in Rome during the 5th century. Paganism was now banned; the temples were closed. The Pope ordered an obelisk from the tomb of Augustus to be erected behind the Basilica, using the power of its monuments to indicate that the Church was the successor to pagan Rome.

wealth and grandeur – a blizzard of gold, mosaic and marble. The new religion was triumphant.

To the rear of the Basilica is an obelisk, one of a pair from the Mausoleum of Augustus, in his day the most powerful man in Rome. The other was, appropriately, set up in front of the Quirinal Palace, the residence of the most powerful man in Rome in later times, the pope, and now home to the president of the Italian Republic. In front of the Basilica a great statue of the Virgin Mary stands on top of a 15 m-high (49 ft) column brought here in 1614 from the Basilica of Maxentius. The inscribed base tells how the Pope took the 'neglected' column, which had once held up a temple of a false god at the command of Caesar, in order to support the mother of the true God.

When this basilica was built, the great imperial basilicas such as Julia, Aemilia and that of Maxentius (Constantine) in the Forum Romanum were all still standing, most of them still functioning. Yet all of these, along with the other great Christian

Opposite: The interior of Santa Maria Maggiore, both in its layout and decoration, gives a sense of the great aisled basilicas of ancient Rome. In the nave were square mosaic panels showing scenes from the Old Testament – here, Lot and Abraham part ways – with people in 5th-century clothing.

Above: This mosaic from the triumphal arch, shows the holy city of Jerusalem (*Hierusalem*) and, standing in front of it, six sheep or lambs, perhaps representing the disciples of Christ. Another six stand in front of the city of Bethlehem on the other side of the arch.

basilicas, such as St Peter's and St Paul Outside the Walls, have been damaged, destroyed or transformed. Santa Maria Maggiore remains, a glimpse of late antique Rome, and a key to the original appearance of older, and incredibly, even grander monuments.

As the 5th century progressed, following a 'last gasp' of weak emperors and 'regencies' by Germanic warlords (some of whom were much more capable than the Romans), the last Western emperor, Romulus Augustulus, was deposed and exiled in AD 476. Between the 470s and 530s Rome was ruled by Germanic Gothic kings, notably Theoderic the Great (r. 493–526). Though continuing to reside in Ravenna, they tried to maintain the urban fabric and revive the civic glory of Rome, making repairs to public monuments including the Colosseum, the theatres, baths and city walls. They put on spectacular entertainments in the Colosseum and Circus Maximus – and even tried to preserve some life-sized bronze statues of elephants near the Forum. The writings of Theoderic's secretary, Cassiodorus, give a glimpse of conditions at this time. There were probably no more than around 100,000 people in Theoderic's Rome, and Cassiodorus marvels at the enormous scale of the monuments, at how vast the earlier population must have been, and at the supplies needed to feed them.

The Byzantine emperor Justinian's attempt to oust these Gothic rulers led to the disastrous Gothic Wars of the 530s–550s, a violent, prolonged and hugely destructive struggle during which the city of Rome was repeatedly besieged and sacked. After this, and the major plague of the AD 540s, Rome's resources were totally depleted and its population had plummeted dramatically, to perhaps as few as 30,000 people. It was effectively the end of Classical Rome. Although imperial control (from Constantinople) continued through the Exarch or Viceroy, power in fact increasingly lay with the popes. The most famous of these, Gregory I 'the Great' (AD 590–604), reigned over a city transformed beyond all recognition from the Rome of only fifty years before.

PHOCAS

(R. AD 602–10)

IT WAS AGAINST this backdrop that the last monument of the Forum Romanum was dedicated in AD 608. The **COLUMN OF PHOCAS** is far from the finest monument, but was so prominent as always to arouse interest.

From AD 608 it carried a gilded bronze statue of the general Phocas, who murdered his way to the throne in Constantinople. The statue was set up by Smaragdus, Exarch (Byzantine governor) of Italy, perhaps commemorating Phocas's gift of the Pantheon to the Pope. The inscription on the plinth states it was erected 'for the countless benefits of his goodness and the calm he brought to Italy' (as distinct from the mayhem he wreaked in Constantinople, including the murder of the emperor Maurice and all his family). Ironically, only two years later, Phocas was himself deposed – stripped naked, dragged through the city and disembowelled – but his Column survived and achieved a certain mystical status. Lord Byron referred to it as 'Thou nameless column with the buried base', reflecting the higher ground level of his time.

The Column, finely made of Greek marble, is 15 m (49 ft) high, stands on a great stepped base, formed of reused architectural blocks, and dates to the 2nd century AD, much earlier than the dedication date. It was probably either moved from a building of that date or already existed as a column monument, perhaps of Diocletian (who erected other honorary columns in the Forum), or of Constantine (who, in Constantinople and elsewhere, used columns as markers in public spaces).

By the time the Column of Phocas was erected, the Forum Romanum, like the city, was a shadow of its imperial self. This

BY THE TIME THE COLUMN OF PHOCAS WAS ERECTED, ROME WAS A SHADOW OF ITS IMPERIAL SELF

The Column of Phocas is the last known pagan monument to be erected in ancient Rome. It was dedicated in AD 608, by the governor of Rome to the Eastern emperor Phocas. By then there was no Western emperor, no Senate and Rome's population had plummeted to under 50,000. Most of the monuments of the Forum Romanum and the city still stood, but they were increasingly vulnerable to nature and man.

almost certainly repurposed gilded statue, set on a repurposed column, situated symbolically in what was once the beating heart of ancient Rome, marked the end of any sense of Classical, as opposed to ecclesiastical, monumentality in the city.

AFTERMATH

From the 6th to 7th centuries, churches continued to be built, restored and endowed, and palaces of the clergy and aristocracy were always needed. But Rome's ancient monuments, abandoned by senators and emperors whose attention and wealth was firmly elsewhere, were now deprived of their real, public impact. Stripped of their context within society, they lost their symbolic worth and meaning. Most of Rome's monuments were now at the mercy of a transformed society that saw structures such as the basilicas and the theatres as, at best, redundant and, at worst, as in the case of the temples, potentially spiritually harmful. And all were increasingly physically decaying and dangerous.

A very few buildings seem to have continued in use – for example the 6th-century AD saw recitals in the Basilica Ulpia – but such mentions in ancient accounts are exceptional. Other buildings that saw continued activity were often used in a very different way. Private houses clustered in the House of the Vestals, and churches took over whole buildings such as the Senate House or the Pantheon, or squatted in once grand structures such as the Basilica Julia and the Temple of Venus and Roma. For most of Rome's monuments it was a story of neglect and slow but sure decay. Wind, rain, frost and vegetation led an assault intensified by fire, flood, earthquake and the growing hunt for building materials. Rubble, silt and fire debris together with composting vegetation and dumped rubbish caused the ground level to rise – in some places tens of feet above the Roman streets.

In this period Rome saw widespread ruralization, with huge areas of the city, including the centre, taken up with agriculture, carried out by people squatting among the ancient monuments. Surprisingly, perhaps, a visitor to Rome in the 9th century saw much of ancient Rome still intact, though eerily empty and clearly in advanced decay. The massive curtain walls of the imperial forums still snaked their way through the monumental centre and the forums themselves were very recognizable. The Forum of Julius Caesar and the Forum of Nerva still had their colonnades and even their temples still largely intact, but each now contained a small village with its houses and farmland. The Temple of Jupiter Optimus Maximus still towered over the city, but as a gigantic ruin. Whole areas of the city were still dominated by massive public buildings such as theatres, arenas and stadiums, near complete, but now transformed into castles and fortified villages surrounded by fields. The mighty Forum Romanum, the heart of the city, became known as the Campo Vaccino, or cow pasture.

'AS LONG AS THE COLOSSEUM STANDS ROME SHALL STAND'

ST BEDE

Yet visitors, usually pilgrims, and writers of itineraries (some of which survive today), still marvelled at Rome's monuments, the technical know-how, the scale, the implied population size. In a sense the emperors' hopes of being remembered through their works lingered for a few more centuries, as some imperial names remained stubbornly attached to their monuments. But Rome now belonged neither to the emperors nor the Senate, but to the popes and Rome's numerous warring noble families.

There were few champions for the remains of Rome's ancient glories, except for some enlightened popes and individuals such as Raphael, but these were exceptional and, as was later proven by the all-consuming hunt for materials for the new St Peter's Basilica in the early 16th century, the monuments, faced with contemporary expediency, would generally not win. As the monuments stood on the brink of the Middle Ages and the Renaissance, they were about to enter their most perilous phase.

And yet, in spite of centuries of abandonment, decay and spoliation, when so very much was lost of imperial monumental Rome, so much still survives. Some buildings, like the Pantheon, require little to complete their evocation of ancient Rome, while others, of which just a few columns survive, make our imagination work harder. But they all speak of imperial glory, of the power of Rome and of the emperors – in Lord Byron's words, 'The dead, but sceptred sovereigns, who still rule our spirits from their urns...'.

If Rome is truly the Eternal City, then above all it is the monuments which make it so. The 8th-century British monk Bede wrote of the great bronze statue or Colossus that stood next to the Colosseum, but here we can surely apply his words to the Colosseum itself and to Rome's monumentality: 'As long as the Colosseum stands Rome shall stand; when the Colosseum falls, Rome too shall fall, and when Rome falls, with it shall fall the world'. It stands.

Overleaf: The German writer, statesman, scientist and traveller Johann Wolfgang von Goethe visiting the Colosseum in around 1790. In 18th-century Europe, anyone of position or culture (though more usually men) included Rome and its monuments in a 'Grand Tour'. The ruins that greeted them were often romantically overgrown, or hidden by later buildings, and many were set in the open farmland which covered much of the ancient city. The Colosseum came to represent the grandeur (and fall) of ancient Rome.

PLAN OF ROME

Rome today occupies a much larger area than the ancient city; the area in grey indicates the boundary line of the Aurelianic Walls (*see* p. 201). All the monuments featured here are accessible to the public without special permit.

1. Temple of Jupiter Optimus Maximus
2. Cloaca Maxima
3. Largo Argentina
4. Temple of Hercules Victor
5. Tiber Island
6. Pons Cestius and Pons Fabricius
7. Republican City Walls (at Termini Station)
8. Forum of Julius Caesar and its Temple of Venus Genetrix
9. Curia
10. Rostra
11. Basilica Julia
12. Temple of Concordia Augusta
13. Temple of Divus Iulius
14. Forum of Augustus and its Temple of Mars Ultor
15. Portico of Octavia
16. Theatre of Marcellus
17. Temple of Apollo Medicus Sosianus
18. Mausoleum of Augustus
19. Ara Pacis Augustae
20. Pyramid of Gaius Cestius
21. Porta Maggiore
22. Domus Aurea and the Colossus of Nero
23. Forum of Vespasian
24. Colosseum
25. Arch of Titus
26. House of the Vestals
27. Stadium of Domitian
28. Forum of Nerva
29. Palace of Domitian
30. Forum of Trajan
31. Circus Maximus
32. Tenement Building
33. Temple of Venus and Roma
34. Pantheon
35. Mausoleum of Hadrian and the Pons Aelius
36. Temple of the Deified Hadrian
37. Equestrian Statue of the Emperor Marcus Aurelius
38. Column of Marcus Aurelius
39. Temple of Vesta
40. Arch of the Bankers
41. Baths of Caracalla
42. Aurelianic Walls
43. Baths of Diocletian
44. Basilica of Maxentius
45. Arch of Constantine
46. San Giovanni in Laterano and San Giovanni Obelisk
47. Temple of Saturn
48. Portico of the Harmonious Gods
49. Santa Maria Maggiore
50. Column of Phocas

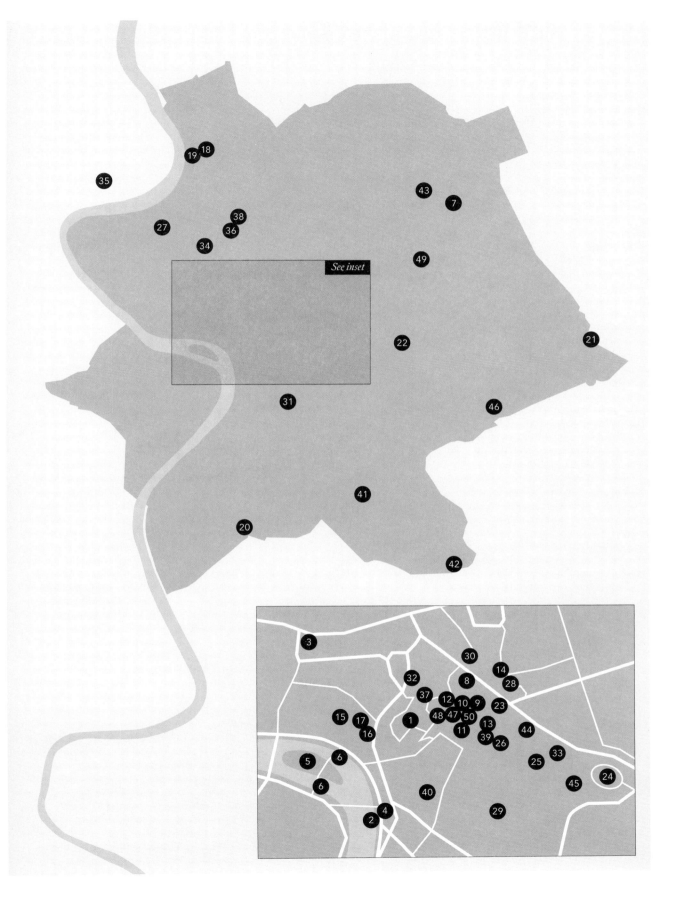

See inset

FURTHER READING

Non-fiction and Reference

Aicher, Peter J., *Rome Alive: A Source Guide to the Ancient City* (Wauconda, IL: Bolchazy-Carducci, 2004)

Angela, Alberto, *A Day in the Life of Ancient Rome* (New York: Europa Editions, 2009)

Beard, Mary, *SPQR: A History of Ancient Rome* (London: Profile Books, 2016)

Beard, Mary, *Emperor of Rome* (London: Profile Books, 2023)

Boardman John, Jasper Griffin and Oswyn Murray (eds), *The Oxford History of the Ancient World* (Oxford University Press, 1986)

Claridge, Amanda, *Rome* (Oxford Archaeological Guides; Oxford University Press, 2010)

Coarelli, Filippo, *Rome and Environs* (Berkeley, CA: University of California Press, 2007)

Connolly, Peter and Hazel Dodge, *The Ancient City: Life in Classical Athens and Rome* (Oxford University Press, 2000)

Davies, Penelope J. E., *Architecture and Politics in Republican Rome* (Cambridge University Press, 2020)

DeLaine, Janet, *Roman Architecture* (Oxford University Press, 2023)

Dey, Hendrik, *The Making of Medieval Rome* (Cambridge University Press, 2021)

Dodge, Hazel, *Spectacle in the Roman World* (London: Bloomsbury, 2011)

Dolansky, Fanny and Stacie Raucci, *Rome: A Sourcebook on the Ancient City* (London: Bloomsbury, 2018)

Dyson, Stephen L., *Rome: A Living Portrait of an Ancient City* (Baltimore, MD: Johns Hopkins University Press, 2010)

Goodman, Martin, *The Roman World 44 BC–AD 180* (London: Routledge, 1997)

Hazel, John, *Who's Who in the Roman World* (London: Routledge, 2002)

Holland, Tom, *Pax: War and Peace in Rome's Golden Age* (London: Little, Brown, 2023)

Hornblower, Simon, Antony Spawforth, and Esther Eidinow (eds), *The Oxford Classical Dictionary*, 4th ed. (Oxford University Press, 2012)

Kelly, Chris, *The Roman Empire – A Very Short Introduction* (Oxford University Press, 2006)

Knapp, Robert, *Invisible Romans – Prostitutes, Outlaws, Slaves, Gladiators, Ordinary Men and Women … The Romans that History Forgot* (London: Profile Books, 2013)

La Regina, Adriano (ed.), *Archaeological Guide to Rome* (Milan: Mondadori Electa, 2004)

Lanciani, Rodolfo, *The Ruins and Excavations of Ancient Rome* (1897; Outlet, 1979)

Lanciani, Rodolfo, *The Destruction of Ancient Rome: A Sketch of the History of the Monuments* (1899; Creative Media, 2018)

Lane Fox, Robin, *Pagans and Christians* (London: Penguin, 1988)

Matyszak, Philip, *Chronicle of the Roman Republic* (London: Thames & Hudson, 2003)

Matyszak, Philip, *24 Hours in Ancient Rome: A Day in the Life of the People who Lived There* (London: Michael O'Mara, 2017)

Millar, Fergus, *The Emperor in the Roman World* (Bristol Classical Press, 1992)

Nicholls, Matthew and Luke Houghton, *30-Second Ancient Rome* (Lewes: Ivy Press, 2014)

Potter, David S., *The Roman Empire at Bay AD 180–395* (London: Routledge, 2004)

Scarre, Chris, *Chronicle of the Roman Emperors* (London: Thames & Hudson, 1995)

Siwicki, Christopher, *Architectural Restoration and Heritage in Imperial Rome* (Oxford University Press, 2019)

Sorrell, Alan and Anthony Birley, *Imperial Rome* (Cambridge: Lutterworth Press, 1970)

Taylor, Rabun, Katherine W. Rinne and Spiro Kostof, *Rome: An Urban History from Antiquity to the Present* (Cambridge University Press, 2016)

Varriano, John, *A Literary Companion to Rome* (London: John Murray Press, 1992)

Woolf, Greg, *Rome: An Empire's Story* (Oxford University Press, 2012)

FICTION

Davis, Lindsey, *The Silver Pigs* (1989)

Davis, Lindsey, *Death on the Tiber* (2024)

Graves, Robert, *I, Claudius* (1934)

Harris, Robert, 'Imperium' trilogy: *Imperium* (2006), *Lustrum* (2009), *Dictator* (2015)

ANCIENT WORKS

Juvenal, *Satires*

Martial, *Epigrams*

Suetonius, *The Twelve Caesars*

SOURCES OF ILLUSTRATIONS

Listed by page number; *a = above, b = below, c = centre, l = left, r = right*

Endpapers: City plan of ancient Rome. Colour lithograph, from Encyclopaedia Britannica, 9th Edition (1875–1889), vol. 20, plate 6. National Library of Scotland, Edinburgh

2 Illustration © Gilbert Gorski; 6–7 Alan Sorrell Archive, no. 760. Artwork by Alan Sorrell © Ashmolean Museum, University of Oxford; 8 Watercolour by Jean-Claude Golvin. Musée départemental Arles Antique © Jean-Claude Golvin/Éditions Errance – Actes Sud. Image created by Daniele Roa; 13 Alan Sorrell Archive, no. 764. Artwork by Alan Sorrell © Ashmolean Museum, University of Oxford; 14 Peter Connolly/akg-images. Image created by Daniele Roa; 16a Image created by Daniele Roa; 16b Photo © Paul Roberts; 17 Alan Sorrell Archive, no. 773. Artwork by Alan Sorrell © Ashmolean Museum, University of Oxford; 18–19 Photo Royal Academy of Arts, London; Photographer Prudence Cuming Associates Limited; 21 Photo Insidefoto di Andrea Staccioli/Alamy Stock Photo; 22 Photo Carole Raddato/followinghadrian.com; 24–25 Rijksmuseum, Amsterdam; 26 Photo © Paul Roberts. Image created by Daniele Roa; 27 Photo © Adrian Constantinescu/Dreamstime.com; 28 Illustration Peter Bull. © Thames & Hudson Ltd; 29a Photo WWE Pictures/Alamy Stock Photo; 29b Photo © Paul Roberts; 30–31 Alan Sorrell Archive, no. 782. Artwork by Alan Sorrell © Ashmolean Museum, University of Oxford; 32 Photo © Paul Roberts; 33 Photo © Sergio Simoes/Dreamstime.com; 34–35 Photo © Sfagnan/Dreamstime.com; 36 Alan Sorrell Archive, no. 780. Artwork by Alan Sorrell © Ashmolean Museum, University of Oxford; 37 Photo © Paul Roberts; 38 Photo Adam Eastland/Alamy Stock Photo; 40 Photo Scala, Florence. Image created by Daniele Roa; 41 Photo RMN-Grand Palais /Dist. Photo SCALA, Florence; 42–43 Museo dei Fori Imperiali, Archivio Fotografico del Museo dei Fori Imperiali. © Rome, Sovrintendenza Capitolina ai Beni Culturali; 44 Photo © Jolanta Wojcicka/Dreamstime.com; 47 Prisma/Album/akg-images; 48 Photo © Jona Lendering/Livius.org; 49 Peter Connolly/akg-images; 50 Photo © Paul Roberts; 52 Balage Balogh/archaeologyillustrated.com/akg-images. Image created by Daniele Roa; 54 The J. Paul Getty Museum, Villa Collection, Malibu, California, 78.AA.261. Digital image courtesy of Getty's Open Content Program. Image created by Daniele Roa; 55 Balage Balogh/archaeologyillustrated.

com/akg-images; 56–57 Illustration © Gilbert Gorski; 59 Photo Bildarchiv Monheim/akg-images; 61 Illustration © Gilbert Gorski; 62a Watercolour by Jean-Claude Golvin. Musée départemental Arles Antique © Jean-Claude Golvin/Éditions Errance – Actes Sud; 62b Photos Trustees of the British Museum, London; 64 Illustration by Peter Bull. © Thames & Hudson Ltd; 65, 66–67 Museo dei Fori Imperiali, Archivio Fotografico dei Museo dei Fori Imperiali. © Rome, Sovrintendenza Capitolina ai Beni Culturali; 68 Photo Hercules Milas/Alamy Stock Photo; 69 The J. Paul Getty Museum, Villa Collection, Malibu, California, 72.AA.106. Digital image courtesy of Getty's Open Content Program; 70 Photo DeAgostini Picture Library/Scala, Florence; 71 Photo Fabrizio Troiani/Alamy Stock Photo; 73 Metropolitan Museum of Art, New York. Harris Brisbane Dick Fund, 1937, Acc. No. 37.45.3(51); 74–75 Photo Scala, Florence; 76 Photo Alinari/TopFoto; 77 Photo © Paul Roberts; 78 Photo Carole Raddato/followinghadrian.com; 79 Photo © Jamie Heath; 80 Watercolour by Jean-Claude Golvin. Musée départemental Arles Antique © Jean-Claude Golvin/Éditions Errance – Actes Sud; 81 Photo © Jona Lendering/Livius.org; 82 Rainer Hackenberg/akg-images; 84–85 Photo © Tinamou/Dreamstime.com; 86 Davide Montalenti/123RF.com; 86–87 Photo DeAgostini Picture Library/Scala, Florence; 89 Photo © Jona Lendering/Livius.org; 90–91 Photo Vito Arcomano/Alamy Stock Photo; 92l Photo Carole Raddato/followinghadrian.com. Image created by Daniele Roa; 92r National Archaeological Museum, Naples. Photo Marie-Lan Nguyen. Image created by Daniele Roa; 93 Photo Giovanni Rinaldi/Shutterstock.com; 94–95 Alan Sorrell Archive, no. 785. Artwork by Alan Sorrell © Ashmolean Museum, University of Oxford; 95 Photo © Jona Lendering/Livius.org; 96–97 © JR. Casals; 98 Photo Giovanni Lattanzi; 99 Photo © Fine Art Images/Heritage Image Partnership Ltd/Alamy Stock Photo; 100 Photo Nicholas Gemini. Image created by Daniele Roa; 102l NY Carlsberg Glyptotek, Copenhagen. Photo Marie-Lan Nguyen. Image created by Daniele Roa; 102r Museo Nazionale Romano (Palazzo Massimo alle Terme), Rome. Photo Scala, Florence – courtesy of the Ministero Beni e Att. Culturali e del Turismo. Image created by Daniele Roa; 103, 105 Museo dei Fori Imperiali, Archivio Fotografico dei Museo dei Fori Imperiali. © Rome, Sovrintendenza Capitolina ai Beni Culturali; 107 Photo Scala, Florence – courtesy of the Ministero Beni e Att. Culturali e

INDEX

*For my dear sister Anne, without whom
this book would not exist, and Sheila, my dear
late sister, who gave me Italy.*

Grazie

ACKNOWLEDGMENTS

The transformation of a ten-page handout for a tour of Rome (from over twenty years ago) into a potential book is entirely thanks to the skill and patience of my dear sister Anne Holmes. With her partner Roger Chubb she spent a great deal of her time transliterating (and translating!) my handwritten additions and annotations. As to the creation of the book itself, huge thanks are due to the amazing team at Thames & Hudson: the wonderful Colin Ridler first encouraged and steered me, launching a project that was taken forward so conscientiously and understandingly by Ben Hayes and India Jackson, and brought to completion with the expert eye of Emma Barton and the skills of Pauline Hubner, Daniele Roa and Robert Heath. At an early stage Carolyn Jones worked her editorial magic and at a late stage Chris Siwicki very kindly agreed to look through the text with a Roman expert eye, saving me from some howlers – any remaining are my responsibility. In my research I was made so welcome by my Rome friends: the British School at Rome, especially Stephen Kay and family, and in particular the late Helen Patterson and her husband Filippo Coarelli. My dear late sister Sheila, who first inspired my fascination with Italy, provided constant support and interest, and last, but by no means least, my husband Richard Tilbrook was my rock, in this as in all.

Frontispiece: a reconstruction of the eastern end of the Forum Romanum looking west towards the Temple of Jupiter Optimus Maximus on the Capitoline Hill.

Pages 6–7: An aerial reconstruction of Rome in the AD 330s, enclosed by the Aurelianic Walls. At the centre is the Colosseum, with the Baths of Caracalla below; left of the Colosseum the Forum Romanum with the Imperial Forums above and the Imperial Palace and the Circus Maximus below. Further left the Campus Martius with the Pantheon and the Stadium of Domitian.

First published in the United Kingdom in 2024 by Thames & Hudson Ltd, 181A High Holborn, London WC1V 7QX

First published in the United States of America in 2024 by Thames & Hudson Inc., 500 Fifth Avenue, New York, New York 10110

Ancient Rome in Fifty Monuments © 2024 Thames & Hudson Ltd, London

Text © 2024 Paul Roberts

British Library Cataloguing-in-Publication Data
A catalogue record for this book is available from the British Library

Library of Congress Control Number 2023945056

ISBN 978-0-500-02568-0

Printed in China by RR Donnelley

FSC www.fsc.org MIX Paper | Supporting responsible forestry FSC® C144853

Be the first to know about our new releases, exclusive content and author events by visiting
thamesandhudson.com
thamesandhudsonusa.com
thamesandhudson.com.au

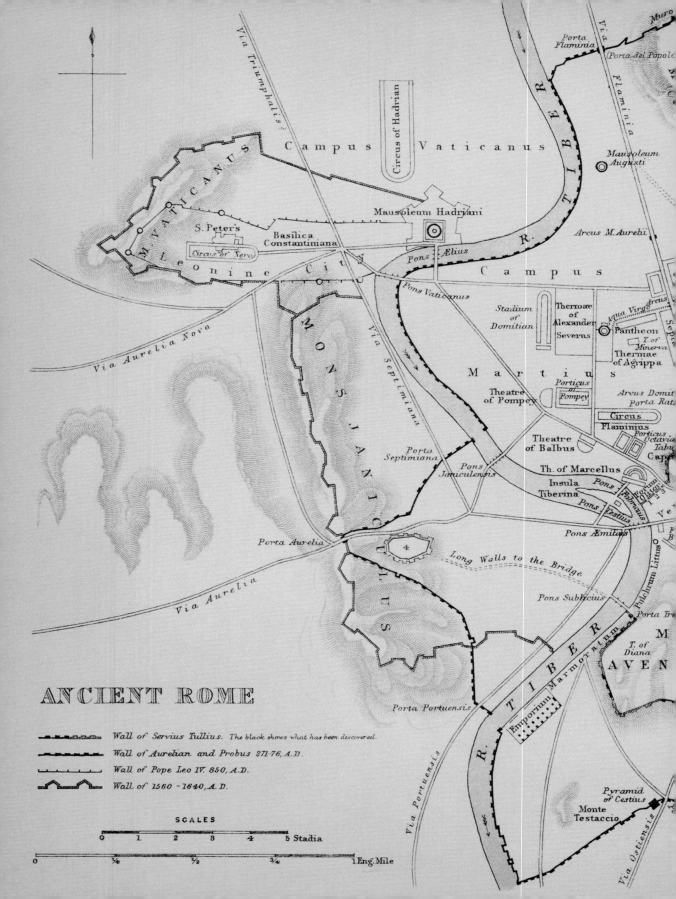

ANCIENT ROME

Wall of Servius Tullius. *The black shows what has been discovered.*
Wall of Aurelian and Probus 271-76, A.D.
Wall of Pope Leo IV. 850, A.D.
Wall of 1560 - 1640, A.D.

SCALES

0   1   2   3   4   5 Stadia

0   ¼   ½   ¾   1 Eng. Mile

Via Triumphalis?

Campus   Vaticanus

Circus of Hadrian

Mausoleum Augusti

Porta Flaminia

Porta del Popolo

Via Flaminia

R. TIBER

Mausoleum Hadriani

Arcus M. Aurelii

M. VATICANUS

S. Peter's

Circus of Nero

Basilica Constantimiana

Pons Ælius

Campus

Leonine City

Pons Vaticanus

Aqua Virgo

Via Aurelia Nova

Via Septimiana

Stadium of Domitian

Thermae of Alexander Severus

Pantheon

T. of Minerva

Thermae of Agrippa

MONS JANICULUS

Martius

Theatre of Pompey

Porticus of Pompey

Arcus Domit. Porta Rat.

Circus Flaminius

Porta Septimiana

Theatre of Balbus

Porticus Octaviæ

Tab.

Cap.

Pons Janiculensis

Th. of Marcellus

Insula Tiberina

Pons Fabricius

Forum

Pons Cestius

Pons Æmilius

Porta Aurelia

4

Long Walls to the Bridge

Pons Sublicius

Pulchrum Littus

Via Aurelia

JANICULUS

Porta Tr.

T. of Diana

AVEN

Porta Portuensis

Emporium

Marmoratum

R. TIBER

Via Portuensis

Pyramid of Cestius

Monte Testaccio

Via Ostiensis